SELF PORTRAIT WITH GREY HAT, 1887   *Stedelijk Museum, Amsterdam*

VINCENT VAN GOGH

A Psychological Study

HUMBERTO NAGERA M.D.

FOREWORD BY ANNA FREUD

INTERNATIONAL UNIVERSITIES PRESS, INC.
NEW YORK

FOREWORD

The letters by Vincent Van Gogh, on which this book is based, have moved the reading public by the sincerity of feeling, the force of expression, the depth of human suffering and the surprising occasional flashes of insight which are displayed in them. If, due to Van Gogh's inevitably one-sided view of events, they do not also forge the links between childhood and manhood, internal and external experience, passion and its moral counterpart, this is precisely what the present author sets out to do. His result is the striking image of a high-minded individual's struggle against the pressures within himself, an image which would command our attention even if the man whose fate is traced were not one of the admired creative geniuses of the last century.

In fact it is the essential conclusion implied by the author that even the highly prized and universally envied gift of creative activity may fail tragically to provide sufficient outlets or acceptable solutions for the relief of intolerable internal conflicts and overwhelming destructive powers active within the personality.

ANNA FREUD

ACKNOWLEDGMENTS

The publishers and author wish to thank Thames & Hudson Ltd, of London and the New York Graphic Society, Connecticut, USA for permission to reproduce extracts from *The Complete Letters of Vincent Van Gogh*.

CONTENTS

CONTENTS

ILLUSTRATIONS

INTRODUCTION

This book is concerned with the life not only of a great painter but of a great man. A psychoanalytic study such as this must of necessity concentrate much of its efforts in the direction of what some will consider the less favourable aspects of the personality, highlighting the various situations of conflict as well as the content of the most essential unconscious phantasies. Because of this it may be felt that the more positive aspects of the personality of the painter are neglected and overshadowed, a view probably based in the misconception that what is 'best' and what is 'worse' in human nature belong in separate compartments and are not as closely interdependent as in fact they are.

I have based the book on the letters written by the painter to his brother and on the additional information contained in *The Complete Letters of Vincent Van Gogh* published by Thames and Hudson. This seemed to me the most reliable source of information available for my purposes. Its publication was supervised first by Theo's wife, and later, by the engineer Van Gogh. I can only recommend its reading to all those who wish to pursue the subject further. References to other sources are stated at the appropriate place.

The letters and numbers that appear in parentheses in the text correspond with the numbers of the letters as they appear in *The Complete Letters*. The reader can in this way easily refer himself to them. The roman numbers correspond to the editorial introduction to *The Complete Letters*.

Very special thanks are due to the painter's nephew, the engineer V. W. Van Gogh, who read the original manuscript and helped in correcting a few inexactitudes. Further, he has generously placed at my disposal valuable additional information.

Finally, I want to express my gratitude to all those who have helped in carrying through this project and especially to my wife, to Mrs A. Hurry, Miss A. Colonna and Mrs M. Cowan.

DR H. NAGERA
London 1966

❧ 1 ❧

BACKGROUND

VINCENT VAN GOGH'S father, the Reverend Theodore Van Gogh, then twenty-seven years old, arrived at the small village of Zundert, in Brabant, Holland, near Belgium, sometime in 1849.

Theo's wife in the introduction to 'The Complete Letters' states that the bachelor parson was very popular among the villagers from the moment of his arrival because of his pleasant appearance and charming ways and was referred to as 'the handsome parson'.

Two years later, in May 1851, he married Anna Cornelia Carbentus. She was thirty-two years of age at the time of her marriage while the Reverend Van Gogh was only twenty nine years old.

By the next year 1852, on March 30th, the first child of their union was born. He was named Vincent Willem Van Gogh but unfortunately he was stillborn.[1] Fate had it that on exactly the same day of the same month, only a year later, their second child was born. He too was named Vincent Willem Van Gogh after the stillborn child, and was to become the famous painter. There was the further coincidence that by pure chance he was inscribed in the parish register of births under the same number as his brother had been a year earlier, that is, number twenty nine. He was to die on the twenty-ninth day of the month of July 1890.

It was Vincent's fate to come into the world without an identity of his own but as a substitute for his dead brother; witness the fact that he was given exactly the same name by his parents.

This dead brother was buried near the entrance to his father's

[1] Another version goes that the child died after a few weeks.

13

chapel at Zundert. Vincent probably saw the grave at least every Sunday. It must indeed have made a strange impression on him, to see his name on the tombstone of his brother.

In assessing the severity of the effects of the loss of his mother's first child, it should be borne in mind that in terms of starting a family she was no longer a young woman: she was thirty-three years old when the first Vincent died.

The replacement of a dead child by another has been a subject of study by a number of psychoanalysts.[1] They have shown that in some families, the parents, after the death of the child become the victims of important psychopathological changes that will profoundly affect and interfere with their relationship to the child whose fate it is to become a substitute for the dead sibling. These parents tend to impose the identity of the child, – who in the meantime becomes highly idealized and the compendium of all their phantasies and hopes – upon his substitute, unconsciously identifying the two siblings. Furthermore the parents are usually unable to accept the substitute as 'the same' with the result that he becomes an increasing disappointment to the parents and naturally, always falls short of the highly idealized image of the dead sibling. The personality development of many such children becomes in consequence greatly affected and distorted. In addition such parents, especially the mothers, are not infrequently panic-ridden by phantasies of the substitute child dying too, which leads to an abnormal concern and oversolicitous attitude towards him. The child, on the other hand, acquires a conviction of his inadequacy and vulnerability in a world of constant unpredictable dangers (Cain). Vincent's anxiety when away from home at some points in his life was no doubt partly determined by these circumstances. Their impact on his personality left clear imprints. We will have to come back repeatedly to this subject later on.

It should be further noted that both Vincents were named not after their father but after their two grandfathers and after a successful and rich uncle, the art dealer Vincent Van Gogh, who was, among the siblings of the Rev. Van Gogh, the closest one to him.

The paternal grandfather, the Rev. Vincent Van Gogh, did his

[1] See for example, Cain, Albert C., and Cain, Barbara S., 'On Replacing a Child', *Journal of the American Academy of Child Psychiatry*, Vol. 3, No. 3, July, 1964.

theological studies at the University of Leiden. He is said to have possessed a strong sense of duty and great intellectual capacities that won him many testimonials as a student. He was born in 1789 and died in 1874. He was married in 1810 to Miss E. H. Vrydag. He lived most of the time at Breda. Little is known of his relationship to the painter.

It is of interest to note that a great uncle of the painter's grandfather was by profession a sculptor. He seems to have been the first member of the family concerned with art. He was successful economically and died single. It was through a legacy of this great uncle of the painter's grandfather that the latter was able to pursue his theological studies at Leiden. Curiously enough his name was Vincent too.

The Reverend Vincent Van Gogh, the painter's grandfather had twelve children, five girls and seven boys, one of whom died in infancy. These eleven paternal uncles of the painter were quite successful in life.

His Uncle Johannes became a Vice-Admiral. Vincent stayed at his house in Amsterdam for some time in 1877.[1] Three of the uncles were art dealers, the eldest, Hendrik, whom Vincent referred to as Uncle Hein in the letters, had a business in Rotterdam and settled finally in Brussels. Cornelius Marinus, referred to as C.M., was the head of the well-known Amsterdam firm of art dealers C.M. Van Gogh. The third uncle, Vincent Van Gogh, had the closest relationship to the painter's father and his family. He started in a little shop in The Hague that soon grew into a well-known art gallery. Later he became a partner in the house of Goupil & Co. in Paris. It was in the firm of Goupil that Vincent and Theo took their first steps in the art-dealing business the latter remaining in the firm till his death.

Uncle Vincent was obliged to give up his active partnership when fairly young because of ill health, but by that time he was in possession of a sizable fortune; nevertheless he remained connected financially with Goupil & Co. After his retirement from the active life of Paris he came to live at Prisenhage, near his father in Breda and his favourite brother the Rev. Van Gogh in Zundert. He possessed a rare collection of paintings and the young Vincent and his brother Theo probably saw their first pictures there. His uncle Vincent and his father (Theo) differed by only one year in

[1] See the Amsterdam Period.

age, and there was the further tie between them that their wives were sisters. Further, uncle Vincent had no children of his own and it seems that his nephew and namesake Vincent, was expected to follow in his uncle's footsteps and eventually to succeed his uncle in the firm, possibly becoming his heir. It was he who decided that when the painter was sixteen years old, he should enter the art dealing business at the house of Goupil & Co., at The Hague. He followed Vincent's life vicissitudes for some time but grew more and more disappointed in his nephew and finally completely turned his back on him.

At the time of his uncle's death Vincent was to say, 'The impression it makes on me is very strange, because in my mind there is an image of the man made up of memories of so long ago, of a great many years ago, and I think it so peculiar that a man one once knew at such close range should have become such a stranger'. (W.4)

Two of his aunts were married to generals in the Dutch army, the other three remained single.

Only the painter's father became a parson like his own father. He is described as a nice man, but not gifted as a preacher, leading a rather obscure life in the ecclesiastical world, always in charge of small country villages.

He started his ecclesiastical career at Zundert, at present a small village of six thousand inhabitants of which only one hundred and twenty or so are protestants. There was even less than that number in the Reverend's time. Zundert was thus an obscure position indeed. Later on he was transferred to Etten, Helvoirt and finally to Nuenen where he died suddenly in March 1885, an event that was to play a most significant role in Vincent's life.

The influence of Vincent's father's profession on him and on his ideals was very great and will be discussed at the appropriate points. He was not a minister of the Calvinistic Creed but belonged to the Gromingen party, a rather moderate section of the Dutch Reformed Church.

Vincent's mother, Anna Cornelia Carbentus, was born at The Hague in 1819, the daughter of a well-known bookbinder. Her married life to the Rev. Van Gogh was, in Theo's wife's opinion, very happy. She is said to have shared her husband's work with all her heart. She had a deep love of nature and could express her thoughts on paper with great facility. She liked to work for the benefit of others. She showed some ability at drawing, an activity

WOMAN PEASANT DIGGING POTATOES

incent's sympathy and affection for the peasant, the poor, and all those who
ffered a hard life shows in many of his drawings of which this is a beautiful
ample. By means of slight distortion of the figure (notice for example her
et) he gave them a living presence and an intense feeling of warmth and
manity. (See Chapter 10, His Father's Death, page 97.)
hoto by courtesy of the Amsterdam Municipal Museum

3. SELF-PORTRAIT

In this one as in several other portraits, Vincent appears with a bandage
covering his mutilated ear. This picture was painted shortly after his
first mental breakdown at Arles.
Photo by courtesy of The Courtauld Institute Galleries, London

that was customary for girls of her time, and it seems quite probable that Vincent's early interest in drawing was the result of an identification with his mother and an attempt at pleasing her and gaining her favour. Be that as it may, there is plenty of evidence that Mrs Van Gogh's relationship to her son Vincent had two sides to it and that many negative aspects permeated it. She most certainly did not think much of her son's work, though occasionally a small compliment appears in her letters to Theo in relation to some drawing of Vincent's. When she moved away from Nuenen, a year after her husband's death, Vincent's paintings were packed in cases and totally forgotten, with the result that the carpenter at Breda in whose care they were left sold everything after several years to a junk dealer! She showed at times little understanding of Vincent's disturbances and difficulties and was obviously disappointed by him, as some passages from her letters will show.[1] She survived the death of her three adult sons and died at the age of eighty-seven.

One of the daughters of another maternal aunt (Sophie Carbentus) married the famous Dutch painter, A. Mauve who greatly influenced Vincent during the Hague period.

Vincent the oldest of those who survived, had five other siblings. When he was two years of age a baby sister was born, his first living rival for the parent's affection. It is not without interest to read that this sister's memories of him refer to his teasing ways with her. Two years later, on May 1, 1857, a boy was born who was named after his father, Theodorus (Theo). This brother and Vincent are said to have been strongly attached to each other from early childhood. Theo always remembered the delightful games that Vincent used to invent that on one occasion led the siblings to give him the most beautiful rosebush in the garden as a present. This special relationship between Theo and Vincent cannot but remind us of the special relationship between their father and uncle, Theo and Vincent again, a relationship that may have contributed to pattern that of the two boys. Theo had to some degree identified with and adopted his uncle Vincent's role as a successful art dealer (he was only twenty-five when he was already at the head of the branch of Goupil & Co. in Paris), while some of Vincent's identifications were more in line with the unsuccessful father as will be shown later.

[1] p. 92.

The relationship between the brothers remained for life something of a very special nature indeed and we will have the opportunity to observe it develop and unfold step by step. Among all the members of the family only Theo was convinced that his brother was a man of some genius, destined perhaps to great things and certainly belonging in a group apart from ordinary people.

After Theo came a sister, Elizabeth, who is hardly ever mentioned in the correspondence. She married a du Quesne and published her reminiscences about her brother around 1910. Elizabeth was followed by a sister Wilhelmien, the younger of Vincent's sisters, who is said to have become schizophrenic in the later part of her life. He referred frequently to her, especially after the Arles period. He kept up a sporadic correspondence with this sister which has been preserved.

Finally, there was the youngest brother, Cornelius (Cor) with whom Vincent had relatively little contact, though he occasionally, while staying with his parents in later years, referred to having gone for walks with him. Still later, in one or two letters to Theo, one finds a couple of passages where it is not difficult to detect some feelings of jealousy because of the attention and concern that his parents were giving to the question of Cor's future and further education. In the end Cor went away from home working for some time as a mechanic with the South African Railways and Goldmines. He died while a volunteer in the Transvaal army.

Vincent as an adult was described by his sister-in-law as reddish haired, of medium height, broad shouldered and giving an impression of strength and sturdiness.

As a small child he was said (by his sister-in-law) to be difficult in temper, troublesome and self willed. He found nature, animals and flowers attractive from an early age. He made all kinds of collections. When he became rough after mixing with the village schoolboys a governess came to help with the children. This servant girl was with the Van Goghs for about a year and a half. When interviewed many years after the artist's death she described Theo as ordinary while she thought Vincent unusual, not like anyone else; he had funny unpleasantly eccentric manners and was punished for it. Vincent was, to her, the least pleasant of the children in the family. She had remained totally unaware of his fame. His sister Elizabeth described him when a boy as a stranger to his mother and sisters as well as to himself. She said that he liked fishing, looking for birds' nests, and hunting beetles and cockchafers of which he made orderly collections. People frequently remarked about his 'strangeness'. He was already somewhat withdrawn and frequently solitary.

The clergyman's carpenter described, after Vincent's death, how the boy used to watch him whenever he came to work at the vicarage. Furthermore he did some very pretty pieces of carpentry himself that gained him the praise of the carpenter.

He used to do some drawings and water-colours at least from the age of eight onwards. These drawings and water colours, according to Vincent's nephew, the engineer Van Gogh, closely resemble in some cases the style of his mother's and may well have been copied from them. A few examples of them (and of his mother's) are to be found in *The Complete Letters of Vincent Van Gogh*. Another drawing entitled 'Farm and Wagon-Shed' appears reproduced in Tralbaut's, *Van Gogh, A Pictorial Biography*. It was drawn by Vincent when he was eleven years old, on the occasion of his father's birthday in 1864.[1]

Theo's wife too described how at eight he had modelled a clay elephant that was praised by the family, a fact that disturbed the little boy to such an extent that he felt compelled to destroy it. A drawing of a cat underwent a similar fate for the same reasons. This reaction is in some ways the clear precursor of a number of conflicts around his work that we will have the opportunity to discuss at a later stage, especially in the chapter dealing with 'The Fear of Success and the Fear of Failure'.

Similarly we should note that these childhood drawings, some of which are dated 1863 (he was ten at the time), are signed with his full name, in contrast with his later work as a painter that was signed only with his christian name Vincent.

At the age of twelve he left home for boarding school in Zevenbergen where he remained four years till the age of sixteen.

This first separation from home and the family was to prove an

---

[1] Furthermore, the engineer Van Gogh has told the author that lately a number of drawings (sketches) have come to light from the time when Vincent was ten years old. Similarly a booklet with sketches of flowers and animals had been discovered. Vincent drew them at the age of twenty for the five years old daughter of his boss Tersteeg at The Hague. There are as well a couple of small drawings of this little girl, her baby brother and a peasant woman (all about 2 × 2 inches). It all goes to show, as the engineer Van Gogh told me, that Vincent was no novice at drawing.

event of great consequence. Vincent had great difficulties about separating and being away from the family that passed unnoticed at this point but of which we will find a great deal of evidence later on. Many years later he described the scene in a letter to his brother. He wrote that it was an autumn day when he stood on the steps on the school watching the carriage that took his mother and father back home, 'One could see the little yellow carriage far down the road – wet with rain and with spare trees on either side running through the meadows'. (82a)

He similarly described how moved he felt a fortnight later when the father came to visit for the first time.

At school he does not seem to have made any particular impression since his teachers, when interviewed about him in their very old age, were not able to remember anything about him. He usually went home on his mother's birthday and one of his sisters recalled how much fun they had then.

By the age of sixteen the question of his profession in life was considered and he was sent to The Hague branch of Goupil & Co. as an apprentice art dealer.[1] This period of his life will be described in the next chapter.

---

[1] It is very regrettable that there are no further reliable sources of information about his childhood.

❧ 2 ❧

VINCENT THE ART DEALER
The Hague Period: July 1869 – June 1873
AND
HIS FIRST DISAPPOINTMENT IN LOVE
The London Period: June 13, 1873 – May 18, 1875

VINCENT joined the firm of Art Dealers Goupil and Co. at The Hague at the age of sixteen years on July 30, 1869. He remained in The Hague for about four years, until the middle of June 1873, when he was transferred to London.

Mr Tersteeg, the head of The Hague branch of Goupil, gave him an excellent testimonial and wrote to his parents assuring them that Vincent would be successful in his profession and stating that at the gallery everybody – art lovers, painters and clients – liked to deal with Vincent.

In August 1872 his brother Theo, by then aged fifteen years three months, came to visit him. Theo was still at school at that time. The first letter of Vincent to Theo was written immediately after this visit. This visit and a number of events that followed were to prove highly significant in the later psychological life of Vincent Van Gogh.

In December 1872 Vincent heard that his brother Theo was to become an art dealer too. He wrote to him expressing pleasure and mentioning that they ought to write to each other regularly. It was then that the interesting regular correspondence between the two brothers started. It was to continue up to the time of Vincent's death in July 1890.

In January 1873 Theo, only fifteen years old, went to the Brussels branch of Goupil to be trained as an art dealer.

From this early correspondence it is possible to establish a number of important factors. First of all it is apparent that Vincent felt a lot of sympathy for Theo who as a young boy of fifteen was separated from his home and family; Vincent well knew this feeling himself. He too at sixteen was sent away from home to The Hague to become an art dealer and a man. Furthermore there was at least one other earlier painful antecedent to this separation that was not only deeply felt but that greatly affected him. It was one of the few events of childhood that Vincent was to refer to in his letters to his brother many years later. At twelve he had been sent to a boarding school at Zevenbergen where he was to stay up to the age of sixteen. Many years later he described to Theo with great effect, his feelings as at Zevenbergen he stood watching the little yellow carriage, that took his parents away, disappear far down the road. He was similarly overwhelmed when his father came to visit him a fortnight later.

Though in both these situations Vincent was able to cope with the separations, there is a great deal of evidence, that we shall continue to put forward in what follows showing that they were not only painful events but that they had had the most serious consequences. I have pointed out in the introduction that the reasons for Vincent's difficulties about separating from his family and being away from home are to be found in the abnormal relationship that developed between the mother and the child who substituted for the dead one. When Theo was sent to Brussels Vincent saw himself again in Theo and felt deep sympathy for his brother. But through this narcissistic identification with the younger brother his own old wound became sensitive again and many sleeping conflicts were reactivated.

At this point the correspondence with his brother which he was so eager to start and maintain, fulfilled the double aim of consoling his brother, with whom he identified, and of helping himself out of his newly reactivated conflicts.

He tried to console his brother: 'I heard . . . that you arrived safe and sound at Brussels and that your first impression was good.

'I know so well how strange you must feel in the beginning, but don't lose courage, you'll get on all right . . . What happy days we spent together at Christmas! I think of them so often. You will also remember them a long time, as they were the last days you spent at home.' (3) And: 'I was glad you answered me so soon and that you like Brussels and have found a nice boarding house. Don't lose heart if it is very different at times; everything will turn out all right. Nobody can do as he wishes in the beginning.' (4)

Two months later, in the middle of March Vincent heard that it had been decided to send him to the London branch of Goupil. Vincent, who was now twenty, took the news with resignation, in some ways looking forward to it; nevertheless an undercurrent of sadness and misery about the change is easily discernible to the reader and was quite conscious to him.

While at The Hague Vincent took every opportunity to go back to his family, to the country which he so loved; the ability to do so greatly helped him to cope with his anxiety about being away from home. It was after all a matter of a few hours and a railway journey to find himself back home. From The Hague to home was near enough; from London to home was a totally different matter.

The move to London implied a different country, with a different language, with no friends or relatives nearby and above all without the possibility of frequent visits home during holidays and other festive occasions. Now the distance, the sea, the cost, etc., made such journeys impossible. If he felt the separation and isolation before, this had to become greater and more complete in London. Vincent really wished he could stay at The Hague. He wrote to his brother: 'It will be quite a different life for me in London, as I shall probably have to live alone in rooms [He had been a lodger with friends of the family in The Hague.] I will have to take care of many things I don't have to worry about now.

'I am looking forward very much to seeing London, as you can imagine, but still I am sorry to leave here. Now that it has been decided that I shall go away, I feel how strongly I am attached to The Hague. Well, it cannot be helped, and I intend not to take things too hard.' And he added as a postscript to the letter: 'Theo, I strongly advise you to smoke a pipe; it is a good remedy for the blues, which I happen to have had now and then lately.' (5)

In May he writes, 'Theo, you have no idea how kind everybody here is to me, and you can imagine how sorry I am to have to leave so many friends'. By June 13th he is in London and writes to his brother 'You must be eager to hear from me, so I will not keep you waiting any longer for a letter', as if it were his brother's need and not his own; then a few lines later he expresses openly his wish to communicate with the brother 'I am very anxious for

a letter; write me soon, and tell me how you spend your day, etc.'
He adds in this first letter from London 'Considering the circumstances, I am doing pretty well'. (9) The passage shows how hard
Vincent is trying to cope: he has to attribute his eagerness to get
in touch to the brother. For the next few months he will resort
even in his letters to some form of denial in relation to his feelings
in general and to his loneliness in particular. These attempts
are hardly successful and the feelings that he tries to deny tend
to break through a few paragraphs later or in one of the following
letters. In a similar fashion he will attempt constantly to externalize his own feelings, fears and internal conflicts by attributing
them to his brother or friends.

The following sequence of statements, now become typical,
shows his inner struggle. First: 'I am quite contented here; I
walk a lot and the neighbourhood where I live is quiet, pleasant
and fresh – I was really lucky to find it', immediately followed by:
'Still, I often think with regret of the delightful Sundays at
Scheveningen and other things, but what's the use of worrying?'
And later in the letter: 'How I should like to have you here.
What pleasant days we spent together at The Hague; I think so
often of the walk on the Ryswijk road, when we drank milk at the
mill after the rain . . . And now, I wish you well. Think of me
from time to time and write me soon, it is such a delight to get a
letter.' (10)

In September 1873, Vincent has the news that Theo is moving
from Brussels to The Hague, where he had been before coming to
London. In November he writes, eager to know about Theo's
new position, new home and general impressions. Typically he
says: 'I am all right. I have a pleasant home, and although the
house here is not so interesting as the one in The Hague, it is
perhaps well that I am here . . . You must have had pleasant days
at home [Theo had gone home before moving to The Hague];
how I should like to see them all again. Give my compliments to
everybody that inquires after me. . . .' (12) Again in January 1874
the same sequence, 'I am doing very well here. I have a delightful
home, and it is a great pleasure to me to study London, the English
way of life and the English people themselves. Then I have
nature and art and poetry. If that is not enough, what is? Still,
I do not forget Holland – especially The Hague and Brabant.' (13)
In April he still refers to The Hague as his second home and re-

24

marks on how beautiful it is in England with his typical ambivalent comments. 'If one really loves nature, one can find beauty everywhere. But still I sometimes long for Holland and especially for home.' (16) He starts now planning to go home for a visit. During all this time Vincent always expresses his wish that Theo will write soon. In June he writes 'Lately I took up drawing again, but it did not amount to much.' (17)

In July he is finally able to go home to Hervoirt for a short holiday. It seems though there is little evidence in his letters at this point, that he has fallen in love with Ursula Loyer, the daughter of his landlady in London. Perhaps one of the few hints in this respect is what he wrote to one of his sisters, 'I never saw or dreamed of anything like the love between her and her mother', 'Love her for my sake'. Years later when he falls in love with his cousin Kee he will refer to this episode of his having been in love with Ursula. Unfortunately Ursula was already secretly engaged. In *The Complete Letters*[1] it is further stated that Vincent's character was from this moment onwards greatly changed, he became melancholic, was in a depressed mood and became more and more absorbed in a kind of religious fanaticism. He started to lead a secluded life, living alone in rooms and seeing nobody. He rarely wrote home, which caused great anxiety to his parents.

Though in *The Complete Letters* and in most biographical studies this episode of his disappointed love for Ursula Loyer is given as a turning point in Vincent's life, and though there is no question as to its importance, I am rather inclined to think that a number of other factors too came together at this time to determine Vincent's change of character. First there was the fact that Vincent had been for about a year away from home and this enforced separation has placed a tremendous strain in his psychological resources. The Ursula episode has to be seen against this background. Vincent was in distress and lonely, away from home and was immediately attracted by the close relationship that existed between this daughter and her mother. Vincent longed for such a relationship, as we will have opportunity to verify later on. Since, on the other hand, there was no question of his been able to stay at home in Holland as he would have wanted, the possibility of a close relation to Ursula and her mother was a second best

---

[1] *The Complete Letters of Vincent Van Gogh*, Thames and Hudson, London, 1958, p. 7.

choice open to him. This family must have been especially attractive to his unconscious because Mrs Loyer was herself a curate's widow, and in this sense a very close symbol of his own mother (the wife of a parson too). Unfortunately, it is not possible, because of the lack of more detailed information, to consider the implications in terms of Vincent's oedipus complex, but it is probable that his severe reaction to this episode is partly linked with these factors. Success with Ursula perhaps might have solved his anxiety about having to return to London again. He would have had a home of his own, full of warmth as he dreamt of it, to which he would be returning. This may partly explain the timing of his declaration to Ursula – just before his trip to Holland – and his lack of any awareness as to her secret engagement. One can further assume that Vincent was unconsciously dissatisfied with his visit to his family at Helvoirt though there was nothing at the time pointing in this particular direction. Nevertheless the later history of Vincent's relations to his family, and especially to his father and mother, makes it plausible that the conscious dissatisfaction, jealousy, rivalry and conflicts that were to be expressed openly in later times were already active at an unconscious level. He must have thought (as he indeed did in later years) that the family did not care about his having to be away in London, that they were not able to recognize his distress and his longings for home, in fact that as long as some of the more wanted siblings were around they wanted him away. Furthermore he may have thought that they had not enough sympathy for him even after the disappointment of his love for Ursula; after all a word from father to uncle Vincent now that he was so distressed would have sufficed to keep him in dear Holland and near home. The separation in London followed by this reactivated many old conflicts in Vincent. He could no longer contain them as successfully as he had done in the past and from this moment onwards we will see them move more and more into the foreground.

During his short holiday at Helvoirt with his parents he drew a great deal. His mother wrote at the time about his having done many a nice drawing of the house, stating, 'it is a delightful talent which can be of great value to him'.

On July 21st he wrote to Theo from London. His sister Anna had come with him and would be found a job there. 'It is a great pleasure for me to walk with her through the street in the evening,

I find everything again as beautiful as when I saw it the first time.' (19) On the last day of July he wrote 'Since I have been back in England, my love for drawing has stopped, but perhaps I will take it up again some day or other.' (20) He had instead started to read a great deal, a habit that would accompany him for many years to come.

Letter 21, written in August, already showed clear signs of his religious fanaticism. There was then a gap in the letters from August 1874 to February 1875. He then commented, 'I do not think you will soon have a chance of being transferred to the house in London' (23), thus expressing a wish to be together with his brother. It was to reappear years later when Vincent was at Drenthe and urged Theo to come to live with him and to become a painter like himself.

In May of the following year he complained that this uncle C.M. and Tersteeg (head of The Hague branch) had been in London. He was hurt that they did not come to see the place where he lived. 'In my opinion they went too often to the Crystal Palace and other places where they had nothing in particular to do. I think they might just as well have come to see the place where I live. I hope and trust that I am not what many people think I am just now.' (26)

In the next few months several deaths occurred which concerned Vincent. First, the thirteen-years-old daughter of his landlady died. He sent Theo a drawing he made the morning the child died, sketched on the title page of *Poems* by Edmond Roche. One of them reads 'I have climbed, sad and alone, the sad and barren dune where the sea laments incessantly, the dune where the billow with its large folds comes to die, monotonous path with tortous windings.' (25) His cousin Annette Haanebeck dies and his uncle Jan Carbentus too died in August.

❧ 3 ❦

THE ART DEALER
BECOMES A TEACHER
The First Paris Period: May 1875 – March 1876
AND
THE BEGINNING OF HIS
RELIGIOUS VOCATION
The Ramsgate and Isleworth Period:
April 1876 – December 1876

VINCENT was now sent to Paris where he stayed for about eight weeks. It was clear that he no longer wanted to be an art dealer. He talked to his uncle Vincent during one of his visits to Paris, asking him if there was any possibility of Theo's coming to Paris but the uncle thought it better for Theo to remain in The Hague.

It is of interest to note that with the exception of Vincent's sudden fanatical religious leanings there are not many signs in his letters pointing to the severity of his disturbances in terms of his actual behaviour. This was by now quite abnormal and led later on to his dismissal from the house of Goupil.

Several things are nevertheless noticeable in the letters from this period, he starts to refer frequently to his father in an increasingly idealized and admiring way that points to an increase of conflicts around him and the mechanisms used to cope with it. There are, in contrast to the frequent references to the father, only very occasional references to the mother. Similarly, he will often send small presents to his father but only rarely to his mother. Furthermore, he starts to compare himself and others unfavourably with his father.

He asks Theo more and more to write to him as much as possible and about everything, and starts to advise him constantly about going to church, reading the Bible, getting rid of certain books, etc.

He wants both himself and Theo to reach perfection. A preoccupation starts to show itself in relation to leading a healthy life and eating healthy food. He advises Theo as to what to eat, about walks, about getting up early in the morning and going to bed early in the evening, etc.

Around November Vincent met a young Englishman by the name of Gladwell, a fellow employee eighteen years old, the son of an art dealer in London. Gladwell was living in the same house as Vincent and they came home together from work. Vincent read to him from the Bible. Gladwell waked him every morning between five and six and prepared breakfast for him. Vincent started to use this boy, expressing through him many of his own inner conflicts, to externalize them. We should further notice the role that the oral (passive-receptive) elements played in this relationship. From now onwards such elements were to become very marked and important in his relation to others. Vincent wrote to Theo. 'My worthy Englishman prepares oatmeal every morning . . . How I wish you could taste it with us.' The externalization of his own inner conflicts is clearly shown in what follows: 'I am so glad that I met this boy. I have learned from him and in return have been able to show a danger that threatened him.

'He had never been away from home, and though he did not show it, he had a sickly (though noble) longing for his father and his home.

'He longed for them with a longing that belongs only to God and to Heaven. Idolatry is not love. He who loves his parents must follow their footsteps in life. He understands this now clearly, and with sadness in his heart, he yet has courage and eagerness to go forward.' (45)

This letter is indeed significative. Vincent has of course no conscious awareness at this point that he is seeing and describing himself in this description of Gladwell. As we will see, his love and admiration for his father, already on the increase, will reach the level of idolatry. The letter further shows the nature of the conflict and a possible attempt at its solution. This conscious and overt admiration of his father is the expression of an unconscious and rather conflictive homosexual passive surrender to the all-powerful father. This passivity, Vincent says to Gladwell, can be acceptable only if expressed in the relationship to God but not to the father. Vincent is indeed moving fast in this direction, his obsession with religion is increasing to the point of a mania. It will lead him finally to attempt to follow on the footsteps of his father by trying to become a parson. Thus he will be surrendering his whole self to the supreme being, to God (the father). This is an attempt at sublimation of his strong bisexual conflict and passive homosexual strivings towards his father.

These conflicts were to prove of paramount importance on his later life but we can not decide at this point the true and basic nature of this bisexual conflict. Is it a primary one, based on the strength in his constitution of the passive-feminine elements, or is it a defensive position to which he has withdrawn as the result of conflictive positive feelings towards his mother – that is, as a defence against his positive oedipus complex? We will leave the question open at this point and come back to it at a later stage when further information may help us to clarify the issue.

I must point out that by now, in psychoanalytic terms, an important regression to the anal-sadistic stage had taken place in Vincent's personality and had so far influenced negatively his ability to relate to other people.

At a later stage it will go even further and show itself for example in his wearing dirty clothes but whatever else this regression may have already affected and will affect later on, it certainly has already severely damaged Vincent's capacity for object-relationships. He had become rude to customers and criticised their taste about pictures, till in the end nobody wanted any dealings with the 'Dutch peasant' a marked contrast with The Hague period when everybody was delighted with him. Further, he told his employers that the art business was nothing but an organized racket. Clearly his reality adaptation perhaps even his reality-testing were empoverished to levels more in line with borderline and psychotic disturbances than with extremely severe neurotic regressions.

Furthermore the need for certain forms of oral gratification and consolations became manifest. Early in December Theo fell in the street and seriously hurt his foot. Vincent wished he could be with him but this was impossible; instead he sent his brother as a consolation some chocolate. (47) Around this time he had again taken to smoking a pipe. 'I refound in my pipe an old faithful friend, and now I suppose we shall never part again.' (48)

In January 1876 Vincent writes to Theo the news that he has been asked to leave the house of Goupil by the following April.

The news is not unexpected: 'in a sense I have done things that have been very wrong, and therefore I have but little to say'. (50) A few days later he writes that his friend Gladwell, who later on will take Vincent's place at Goupil, is moving from Vincent's lodgings. Vincent is very sorry about it. 'We feel lonely now and then and long for friends and think we should be quite different and happier if we found a friend of whom we might say, *He is the one*. But you, too, will begin to learn that there is much self-deception behind this longing; if we yield too much to it, it would lead us from the road.' (52) The sublimated homosexual aspects of the relationship to this younger boy can not escape anybody. The news of his oncoming dismissal and of Gladwell's move (though he still came on Fridays to read poetry with Van Gogh) further affects Vincent who increasingly seeks refuge in his religious feelings and readings. He has read *Scenes from Clerical Life* and was very struck by the last story, 'Jane's Repentance'. Vincent's unconscious identification with the clergyman in the story is going to give shape soon afterwards to several years of his life. The story concerns the life of a clergyman who lives in close contact with and devoted to the needs of the poor inhabitants of a town. For dinner the clergyman will have nothing but underdone mutton and watery potatoes. He dies at thirty-four after being nursed during a long illness by a woman who was a drunkard who through his teaching and support had conquered her weakness. Vincent is a good replica of the clergyman in this story when he is a few years later completely devoted to the miners at the Borinage in Belgium, in his capacity as an evangelist parson. Vincent too was to have a close relationship to a drunken prostitute (Christine) whom he wanted to rescue from the street and to give a home.

Dismissed from Goupil at the beginning of April he went to Etten to his family. By April 17 he was back in England at Ramsgate where he had found a position as a teacher. He was to have no salary for a month but was 'glad' to have found something and at least to have board and lodgings. Mr Stoke's school was moved in June to Isleworth but Vincent left there in July since Mr Stokes could not pay him a salary. He went then to another school run by Mr Jones, a Methodist clergyman.

This new enforced separation from his family, again to England, reopened his wounds and Vincent expressed his feelings quite openly in a letter to his father and mother. 'In thought we will stay together today. Which do you think is better . . . the joy of meeting or the sorrow of parting? We have often parted already; this time there was more sorrow in it than there used to be . . . And didn't nature seem to share our feelings, everything looked so grey and dull a few hours ago . . . These first hours after our parting . . . how we are longing for each other . . .' He recounted how when the train taking him away from Etten passed through his old boarding school he 'thought of the day you took me there and I stood on the steps at Mr Provily's, looking after your carriage on the wet road; and then of that evening when my father came to visit me for the first time. And of that first homecoming at Christmas!' (60)

In August Harry Gladwell's sister met with a fatal accident. She fell from her horse and after five hours of unconsciousness she died. Vincent arrived there after a six-hours' walk, just when the family returned from the funeral, 'It was indeed a house of mourning, and it was good to be with them. I felt a kind of shyness and shame on witnessing that great impressive sorrow'. There can be little doubt that in Vincent's unconscious he was reliving again his memories and phantasies of the sadness, the sorrow of his parents and especially that of his mother, at the loss of his elder brother. He added: 'How I wish to comfort that father, but I was embarrassed before him; to the son I could speak. There was something holy in that house yesterday.' (73)

By October Vincent had an intense longing to go back home and to see his family. He wrote to Theo: 'But how I should like to be with you, Oh why are we all so far away from each other . . . but how can it be helped?' (74) Four days later again, 'How I long to see you again, Oh, my longing is sometimes so strong.' (76) And 'How little we see of each other and how little we see of our parents, and yet so strong is the family feeling and our love for each other that the heart uplifts itself . . .' (78) 'But, boy, how I am longing for Christmas and for you all; it seems to me I have grown years older on these few months.' (74)

By December he was back at home at Etten with his parents. He was not to come back to England any more since there were no opportunities for him there. He wrote to Theo 'There are many things that make it desirable, the being back in Holland near Father and Mother, and also near you and all the others . . . How often have we longed to be together, and how dreadful is the

is first great masterpiece of which there are several versions. They were painted shortly ter the death of his father, as if his talents were then suddenly liberated. His beloved easants eat the fruit of their efforts in their modest hut. Curiously enough the clock stands ill (now forever) at twenty five to twelve. Added up they make thirty seven, the age of his uicide and death. Another numerical coincidence in the life of the painter that has to be lded to the many other numerical coincidences referred to in the text. (See Chapter 10, is Father's Death, page 96; Chapter 20, Vincent's Suicide, page 181 and Chapter 1, ackground, page 13.)

hoto by courtesy of the Amsterdam Municipal Museum

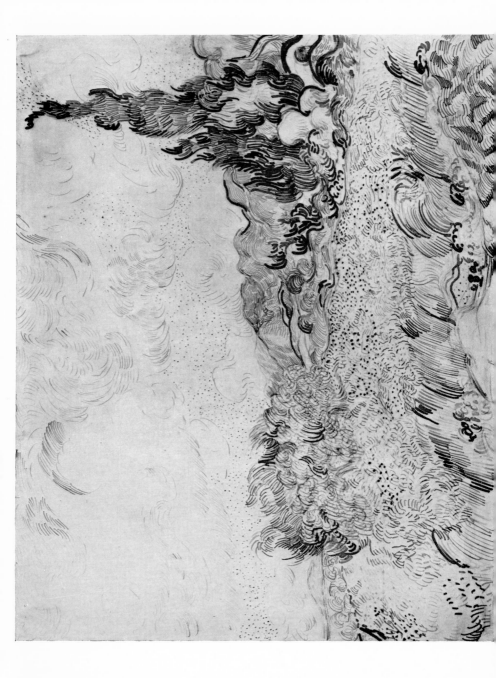

Vincent was fascinated by the cypress, the majestic symbol of death that he reproduced in many of his drawings and paintings of this period. The end was now getting closer. (See Chapter 20, Vincent's Suicide, page 174.)
Photo by courtesy of the Amsterdam Municipal Museum

feeling of being far from each other in times of illness or care . . . and then the feeling that want of necessary money might be an obstacle to coming together in time of need.' (83) And, 'sometimes I feel so delighted that we are living again on the same soil and speaking the same language'.

During the time in England Vincent's religiosity had been increasing quite rapidly. He had been permitted occasionally to preach in place of Mr Jones and there is preserved from this time a long sermon he had prepared and delivered to the congregation. The following passage in his sermon is of interest 'Has any one of us forgotten the golden hours of our early days at home, and since we left that home – for many of us have had to leave that home and to earn their living and to make their way in the world.' His letters to Theo were similarly full of religious comments and quotes from the Bible.

≈ 4 ≈

VINCENT THE BOOKSELLER AND HIS RELIGIOUS MANIA
The Dordrecht Period: January 21, 1877 – April 30, 1877

VINCENT now went as an assistant to a bookshop at Dordrecht where he remained only for about three months (January 21, 1877 to April 30, 1877). There he was a boarder at Mr Rijken's house with several others. His room-mate was Mr P. C. Görlitz, then a young schoolmaster.

He was employed in Blusse and Van Braam (the bookshop) by Mr Braat, senior, whose son Franks had business relations with Theo. His uncle Vincent too seems to have helped in securing this position for him.

One of Mr Braat's sons described Vincent (years after his death) as an unattractive boy, always a bit unsociable who hardly spoke a word to anyone in the shop. He thought Vincent was something of a recluse and doubted if anybody in Dordrecht knew him. Mr Rijken, his landlord, described him as a queer chap; occasionally he thought Vincent was out of his mind. He avoided the other lodgers as much as possible and always wanted to be alone. Sometimes he would not come home for dinner and when told that he ought to eat he would reply, 'I am not in any want of any food; eating is a luxury.' He would generally not eat meat, except, perhaps, for a little morsel on Sundays. He was extremely frugal; a few potatoes with a little gravy and some vegetables was his usual dinner. He kept very late hours, reading and moving about in his room. Mr Rijken used to get annoyed with him because he covered the walls with prints and drawings fixed with nails which he ruthlessly drove into the walls.

According to Mr Görlitz, Vincent spent every night reading the Bible, making notes from it and writing sermons. He lived

34

ascetically and his only luxury was his pipe. On a Sunday he used to go several times to church, to the Dutch Reformed, the Jansenist, the Roman Catholic and the Lutherans for example. Görlitz once expressed his astonishment at this behaviour. Vincent answered with a pleasant smile. 'Do you really think, Görlitz, that God cannot be found in the other churches ?' (94a)

At Blusse and Van Braam, Vincent according to Mr D. Braat, had to show the goods to the customers and now and then to deliver some of them. According to Görlitz he kept the books there as well. Vincent was not interested in the least in this work and spent much of his time translating the Bible into French, German, and English, with a fourth column for the Dutch text as well. At other times when people happened to look he would be making little sketches, and pen-and-ink drawings.

During this period at Dordrecht, according to the remarks of various people, he was never angry. On the contrary he was said to be extremely patient. Nevertheless he used to tell customers exactly what he thought of the artistic value of the prints they came to buy. Such behaviour was frequently not in the best interests of his employer, and often irritated customers since he would advise them, for example, to buy a cheaper engraving which he considered more artistic rather than a more expensive one which they might have preferred. It can be argued that this form of behaviour could well be an indirect form of expression of aggression, both against his employers and the customers. Such elements were present no doubt, but it seems that his behaviour in this respect was similarly motivated by the need to be honest and truthful – to what was obviously an absurd degree. It is a further proof of his inability to adapt to reality. To tell the truth, even if it was only the truth as he understood it, was at this point the only possible form of behaviour for him. This type of behaviour contains as well elements derived from his anal regression.

Mr Görlitz described how one afternoon while going for a walk, Vincent suddenly saw a deserted, miserable, street dog. He looked in his pocket and found two pennies. They were all the money he had left since it was near the end of the month. He bought two rolls with one penny to give to the dog, and stood looking at the animal full of complacency. The animal being hungry devoured the bread in an instant. Vincent went back to his companion and said, 'What do you think this animal told me just now? That he would like another couple of rolls like that', and following his impulse, he bought two more and gave them to the yearning dog.' (A7) Görlitz comments that Vincent did not even have the money to buy himself a pack of tobacco, his only luxury.

In February he planned to give his father as a birthday present George Eliot's *Scenes from Clerical Life*, one of whose stories had deeply impressed him, as we have mentioned and on the basis of which some aspects of his life were to be patterned. He was hoping, too, to visit Etten by the eleventh, when his father's birthday would be celebrated in spite of the fact that he had only been away from home for a few days.

Though on the whole when reading Vincent's letters to his brother we see only one side of a dialogue his comments on remarks made by Theo sometimes enable us to reconstruct the full interchange.

One such occasion occurs in Letter 88. Theo apparently had written to Vincent 'I am so sad and so lonely', a sentence that helps us to understand what motivated Theo's correspondence and relationship to his brother at this stage. He, like Vincent, felt at times sad and lonely and may have found great comfort in the correspondence with his brother.

Vincent replied that he too felt like that sometimes but hoped to have his life changed through God. 'It is good to think of Jesus in all places and circumstances . . . You do not know how I am drawn to the Bible; I read it daily, but I should like to know it by heart and to view life in the light of that phrase, Thy word is a light unto my path and a lamp unto my feet [*Sic*. Ps. 119:105]. I hope and believe that my life will be changed somehow, and that this longing for him will be satisfied. I too am sometimes lonely and sad, especially when I am near a church or parsonage.' (88). 'Him' in this context can be seen as a condensation of the idealized 'quasi-God' image of his father and of God as he conceived of it. The longing for him is a sublimated expression in religious terms of unconscious passive homosexual strivings in relation to his father. The identification in his unconscious mind between his father and God needs no elaboration here. It is quite evident for anyone who reads the letters. At the end of this same letter there appears another example of such a connection. He refers now to his father's words as he did above those of God. His father's word is too 'a light unto my path and a lamp unto my feet'. He writes to Theo, 'Hate sin; remember how Father prayed every morning, "Deliver us from evil, especially from the evil of sin," and well he knows.' (88) This letter also contains – as do many of his letters – a condensed version of his oedipal struggles and defensive attitudes. At the end of it, and without any apparent connection with the rest of the text, there appears the following sentence, 'The photograph "Mater Dolorosa" which you sent me is hanging in my room. Do you remember, it was always hanging in Father's study at Zundert?' The unconscious, perhaps conscious connection between this 'Mater Dolorosa' and his mother, who had lost her firstborn child and was consequently a true 'Mater Dolorosa' herself is clear. Furthermore this 'Mater Dolorosa' was the same as the one that his father always had hanging in his study; it was the 'Mater Dolorosa' so to say, that belonged to the father. It is, of course, by no means extraordinary that a man of Vincent's background attempted to deal at this point in his life with his unconscious conflicts by the means of the rich symbolic imagery that religion offers. It presents, as is well known, the unconscious aspects of the human mind, the id, with the right kind of elements on which to displace and express otherwise forbidden conflicts. And religion is often equally as welcome to other aspects of the human mind that is, to the ego, because of the multiple possible ego identifications made available and the innumerable possibilities of sublimation that it opens up. It has been said, and I believe rightly so, that Van Gogh's many unconscious identifications includes an identification with Christ. His behaviour with the miners in the Borinage district supports this view. His mother, like Christ's mother, was a true 'Mater Dolorosa'; his father, 'the handsome parson', from being a man of God, became God himself, the Father, the possessor of the 'Mater Dolorosa'. Who else could Vincent be then than Christ himself, how could he fail to fulfil his 'Father's' purposes for him? It is indeed unfortunate that nowhere is an account to be found of the content of his delusional states when many years later his mental equilibrium did break down. The knowledge of this content would have thrown a much clearer light on the nature of Vincent's unconscious conflicts and psychopathology. We do know nevertheless that his delusions were frequently of a religious character, possibly combined with elements of an obscene nature which greatly tortured him.

He was soon to leave Dordrecht and the bookselling business. His religious longings and call had reached their full intensity. At this point an interesting incident revealed one of his unconscious motives for becoming a parson that is, the wish to take his father's place, a wish that carried deep unconscious implications in terms of his oedipus complex, namely the phantasy of taking his father's place in the relationship to his mother. His father had been unwell and another parson had to preach for him. Vincent wrote 'Father was not well last Sunday, and the Reverend Mr Kam preached for him.' (89) He obviously thought that he could have substituted him in this occasion. Vincent now started to assume without any reason that his father wished him to follow in his steps. Though this was perhaps not an unlikely possibility there is no evidence in his letters that his father had ever explicitly expressed such a wish to Vincent or even to somebody else in Vincent's presence. Our only evidence on this point comes from a remark of A. de Graaf, who was verger of the Protestant Church during the time of the Reverend Mr Van Gogh. According to de Graaf the Reverend Mr Van Gogh would occasionally say to him that 'there was such an extraordinary spirit in Vincent', and that he would have liked so much to make a preacher of him. (165b)

It is of course quite possible that the pastor had such hopes in relation to his first son, the stillborn Vincent, and that in his own mind at least may have had a similar hope for the second Vincent. The lack of positive evidence in this respect forces one to conclude that if the pastor had such hopes at all, he must have found Vincent unsuitable and the possibility unlikely. Be that as it may, Vincent now felt that this was his father's dearest wish. 'I know his heart is yearning that something may happen to enable me to follow his profession; Father always expected it of me, – oh, that it may happen and God's blessing rest upon it.' (89) He continued, 'In our family, which is a Christian family in the full sense of the word, there has been, as far as one remembers, from generation to generation, one who preached the Gospel. Why shouldn't a member of that family feel himself called to that service now, and why shouldn't he have reason to believe that he may and must declare his intentions and look for the means to reach that goal?' (89) He added: 'It is my fervent prayer and desire that the spirit of my father and grandfather may rest upon me, that it may be given to me to become a Christian and a Christian labourer, and that my life may resemble more and more the lives of those named above; for behold, the wine is good, and I do not desire a new one.' (89) This newly-acquired and most pressing ego-ideal embodies in itself many seeds of destruction. It is an extremely high one since it is based not on the reality adapted perception of those (father, uncles, etc.) on which it is modelled, but on his infantile images of them, and consequently on enormously idealized distortions of such figures and of their activities and behaviour in life. Thus he added, 'Whenever I see Uncle Vincent, I am struck anew by something indescribably charming and, I should say, something good and spiritual in him, I do not know what to call it. Father has it even more; Uncle Jan, in another way; and it is also in Uncle Cor. Even in a hundred people you would not always find one like them, so let us carefully treasure their memory and their image.' (104) This ego-ideal carried with it the fear of falling short, the fear of failure that was to haunt him, especially during the Amsterdam period, that was to become his constant companion, expressing itself in a multitude of forms and combinations. It was accompanied by a fear of the criticism of those on whose admiration and approval his self-esteem and well-being were largely dependent, as well as by the fear of the criticism of his severe and strict conscience, his own super-ego. Clearly such an ego-ideal was built up partly on the basis of an intense wish to comply with what he thought to be his parental figures' wishes, and with the hope of gaining their pardon, admiration and love; perhaps even of regaining a feeling of being wanted or at least of placing himself on a similar footing to his siblings in regard to his parents' affection. Vincent, as we will have the opportunity to see later, believed that he was at best considered and treated like his family's dog, in what he felt to be a sharp contrast to the relationship of his parents to his other siblings.

All these elements are clearly perceptible in the following passages written in answer to his brother Theo who had expressed a wish to be 'far away from everything' since he had brought sorrow and misery to everybody (presumably he refers to a love affair with a prostitute). Vincent wrote, 'When I think of the past; when I think of the future of almost invincible difficulties, of much and difficult work which I do not like – which I, or rather my evil self, would like to shirk; when I think of the many watching me who will know where the fault is if I do not succeed who will not make trivial reproaches, but as they are well tried and trained in everything that is right and virtuous and pure gold, the expression on their faces will seem to say, we have helped you and have been a light into you, we have done for you what we could – have you honestly tried? What is our reward and the fruit of our labour now? See! when I think of all this and of so many other things like it too numerous to mention, of all the difficulties and cares that do not lessen as we advance in life – of sorrow, of disappointment, of failure, of disgrace – then I also know how the longing, I wish I were far away from everything!

'And yet I go on . . . believing that notwithstanding everything that seems against me, I yet shall reach the aim I am striving for, and if God wills it, find favour in the eyes of some I love.' (98) And: 'If I may become a clergyman and fill that position so that my work resembles that of our father, then I shall thank God.' (99)

Theo was involved in his love affair and confided in Vincent. There was some question as to the attitude their parents would take if they knew of this relationship and especially if Theo were to carry it through. Vincent, who was completely given over to his father for the time being commented 'your mind will be divided – she or my father – I think our father loves you more than she does – that his love is of greater value'. (90)

At the beginning of April he learned that Aerssen (who worked as a gardener at the parsonage at Zundert) was dying, 'At this news my heart was drawn so strongly toward Zundert that I longed to go there.' (91) Vincent had no money for this journey and had to ask his room-mate Görlitz for a loan. He said to him, 'I'm so fond of that man, and I should like so much to see him once more; I want to close his eyes, but I can't pay for the journey to Breda.' (A7) He arrived very early at the churchyard in Zundert (where his brother was also buried) . . . 'everything was so quiet. I went over all the dear old spots, and the little paths, and waited for the service there. You know the story of the Resurrection – everything reminded me of it that morning in the quiet graveyard.' (91) Aerssen died the night before Vincent's arrival. He wrote, 'Oh! they were so grieved, and their hearts were so full . . . His passing was peaceful. I shall never forget that noble head lying on the pillow. The face showed signs of suffering, but wore an expression of peace and a certain holiness. Oh! it was so beautiful.' (91) Two months later he would write to his brother, 'When I was standing beside the corpse of Aerssen the calmness and dignity and solemn silence of death contrasted with us living people to such an extent, that we all felt the truth of what his daughter said in her simplicity: "He is freed from the burden of life, which we have to carry on still".' (98)

Vincent now wants more and more to dedicate his life to the service of God and the Gospel. His ego-ideal is pressing him ever harder and his whole self-esteem depend on his success or failure in this new endeavour. If successful, he feels all past failures will be forgiven. 'Oh! Theo, Theo boy, if I might only succeed in this, if that heavy depression because everything I undertook failed, that torrent of reproaches which I have heard and felt, if it might be taken from me, and if there might be given to me, both the opportunity and the strength needed to come to full development and to preserve in that course for which my father and I would thank the Lord so fervently.' (92)

An interesting episode took place at this point. He had been anxiously looking for some of his parents' letters dating from the period before he was sent to England which he thought he might have lost. They were found in Aunt Roos' writing desk by Mrs Roos (who had been his landlady). It is possible that his not taking these letters with him to England and forgetting where he had left them was one of the few signs of the unconscious resentment he felt towards his parents for being sent to England. He must have wanted them to intercede with Uncle Vincent so that he could remain at The Hague, though he did not dare to verbalize his anxieties and wishes in this respect because he so wanted to comply and to please everybody. When the letters were found he rationalized his not taking them to England with him in the following way, 'Now I remember quite well that I left it with Roos when I went to England because there was not much room in my trunk and also because I thought it would be safer than taking it with me abroad.' (93) This further shows the conflict about having them lost: by trying at a conscious level to protect them from being lost he in fact forgets completely where he has kept them for safety purposes. Now that he hopes to gain fully the parental approval, and especially that of his father, by becoming a man of God himself, he interprets the refinding of the letters magically. 'It seems to me a new proof and a hint – I have already observed more of them lately – that everything will be all right with me, that I shall succeed in the thing I so earnestly desire. Something of the old faith grows in me that my thoughts will be confirmed, my spirit renewed and my soul restored to the old faith. It will be a choice for my whole life!' (93)

A no less interesting aspect of this episode is Vincent's comparison of the joy he felt when the letters were found with the joy that the 'woman who found her mite again must have felt' thus hinting at some aspects of his unconscious feminine identifications.

In his last letter from Dordrecht there appears towards the end a very illuminating passage as to his later development as a painter. Vincent in his extreme idealization of his father compares his work and life with that of painters he admired greatly, like Breton, Millet, Jacquet, Bosboon and even Rembrandt. He says, 'What a resemblance there is between the work and life of Father and that of those men; I value Father's higher still.' (94) This overvaluation and excessive idealization of his father placing him above the greatest painters had to be completely shattered, before Vincent the painter could be born out of the destruction of Vincent the preacher and his idealized father. Then, and only then, could painting and art be valued beyond and above God and religion. But for sometime still art and priesthood remain closely associated in his mind and heart thus he says, 'I have heard the Reverend Mr Laurillard three times; you would like him too, for it is as if he paints, and his work is at the same time high and noble art. He has the feeling of an artist in the true sense of the word.' (101a)

It is worth noting that after hearing the Reverend Mr Laurillard preaching on 'Jesus walked in the newly-sown field', he wrote of how the Reverend spoke of the parable of the sower and about 'the man who should cast seed into the ground and should sleep and rise, and the seed should spring up and he knoweth not how'. 'He made a deep impression on me.' (101) He was never to preach on such subjects from a pulpit but instead he painted many versions of that 'sower' and of related subjects with a distinctly religious passion.

At some point Mr Görlitz, Vincent's room mate at Dordrecht, visited Vincent's father at Etten to discuss the possibility of taking a teaching vacancy in a little village near Etten. On being questioned by Mrs Van Gogh he explained that Vincent was unhappy and that his only desire was to become a preacher. As

a result it was arranged that Vincent go to Amsterdam to the house
of his uncle the rear-admiral in order to study for his future
career.

✺ 5 ✺

VINCENT THE STUDENT
The Amsterdam Period: May 9, 1877 – July 1878

ONCE in Amsterdam, living at the house of his uncle the rear-admiral, he began to prepare for the entrance examination at the University. He had to study several subjects for this purpose, among them Latin and Greek. His uncle, the Reverend Mr Stricker, found him a teacher – Mendes da Costa – who was to help prepare him for the examinations.

Vincent had been in Amsterdam for only a few days when he made a most interesting slip of the pen in one of the letters. It was to prove prophetic. He tells his brother 'Yesterday I was at the early morning service and heard a sermon on "I shall forever be *at strife with man*" (presumably meaning the text, 'My spirit will not always strive with man'). (96)

During this period Vincent was to witness a sad incident by which, as was to be expected, he was very much impressed. It happened that two children accidentally fell into the water of a canal. Vincent decided to accompany the two ship's doctors sent by his uncle the admiral to help in the rescue. He later went with the men who carried the unfortunate little boy to a drug store where they tried in vain to bring the child back to life. In the meanwhile the father of the child recognized his son's body and the little corpse was carried home. Though he did not know these people he felt compelled during the evening to return to the house: 'That evening I went to see the people once more, it was already dark in the house; the little body was lying so still on a bed in the little parlour, he was such a pretty little boy. The sorrow was great; he had been the light of the house, as it were, and the light had now been extinguished. Though rough people express their

44

sorrow crudely and without dignity like this mother, one still feels deeply in a house of mourning, and the spell remained with me the whole evening while I took a long walk.' (101) Significantly towards the end of the letter he hopes it will be given to him to write a sermon on 'Awake thou that sleepest, and arise from the dead, and Christ shall give thee light'.

We referred earlier to some psychoanalytic studies which demonstrated how the death of a child affected the family and the substitute brother. In Vincent's case the situation had been further complicated by the fact that he was conceived only three months after the death of his brother so that his mother's mental representation of him was developing while she was in deep sorrow and mourning for her first son. Here again the psycho-analysis of mothers in their second pregnancy whose first child was alive had shown the existence of innumerable conflicts of loyalty and of other types in relation to the first-born which had to be controlled and mastered if the relationship to the second child or to both was to develop within normal limits. These difficulties increase one hundredfold and may well become insuperable if it happens that the first has died as was the case here. From the insight gained from such studies one can attempt to reconstruct the psychological state of the painter's mother while she was pregnant with him. She must have felt the usual turmoil of inner contradictions, the usual conflicts of loyalty, particularly because all the hopes and plans for her first-born child had been shattered by fate. She may have felt at times that this new life was that of an ursurper. Was this new child so soon to take the place in her heart of the dead one? Was he to fulfil the same expectations, phantasies and hopes that were aroused in relation to the first conceived? But how could he possibly do this, becoming somebody who was already dead, that he was not really meant to be? Was not this an intrusion in her pain, in the intimacy of feelings, of expectations, of hopes, of plans and longings between a mother and her first conceived child? And how could she think, hope and plan any differently for this second child at such a close range from the death of the first without feeling that she was insulting his memory and was in fact a traitor to it? Similar phantasies even if in a lesser degree must have haunted at least the unconscious mind of the father. It was against this conflictive background of emotional uncertainty, instability, conflictive loyalties, ambivalence, sadness and with-drawal that Vincent was to be born. Perhaps taking this into account, we will not be so surprised at his constant struggle to find an identity for himself in life, an identity in his art belonging only to him, a unique style, that, as he was to say would distin-guish him from everybody else and would make his work recog-nisable even when unsigned. This unique identity he most certainly found through his art in the end.

Can we be surprised at the effect that death, and beyond it the sorrow of those who mourn, had on him?

Many times as on the above occasion he struggled with all his might to understand the very nature of this feeling that his parents experienced and that had especially affected his mother. He may well have come closest to it in his famous drawing 'Sorrow', significantly depicting a naked woman. The model for it was Sien, the prostitute whom he has rescued from the street and who was at that time in fact expecting her second child.

His work in Latin and Greek, needed for his entrance exami-nation to University, was proving rather hard and Vincent was full of anxiety in case he failed yet once more. An allusion to the possibility of escaping it all by means of suicide occurs now, though in a rather jocular way. He writes 'I breakfasted on a piece of dry bread and a glass of beer – that is what Dickens advises for those who are on the point of committing suicide, as being a good way to keep them, at least for some time, from their purpose.' (106)

During this time he had a great deal of contact with his Uncle Stricker, a well-known preacher in Amsterdam. He met Stricker's son-in-law and daughter, Kee Vos, with whom he was to fall in love some time later, soon after she became a widow, an incident of great importance in Vincent's life. He was full of admiration at this point for the Reverend Mr Stricker, who, like his father and other uncles, was highly idealized for a time.

By October his teacher, Mendes da Costa had reported on his progress. The report was not completely negative but there was no doubt that Vincent found the greatest difficulties in formal scholastic work. It still remained for him to tackle 'that terrible Algebra and Mathematics'. (112) He must try hard, *it is a race and a fight for my life* – no more, no less'. (114) By Christmas he was longing to go home and, like a young scholar, hoping that his father would be satisfied with the work he had done so far.

Two months later his father visited him in Amsterdam. He describes to his brother as the most pleasant recollection of the father's visit 'a morning we spent together in my little room, correcting some work and talking over several things'. (118) This ideal picture of his father and himself harmoniously together was dear to Vincent's heart. He had made many a compromise within himself in an effort to achieve it. One is reminded of how a few months earlier he had bought a lithograph representing 'an old and young clergyman talking together in a garden. (112)

At the time of his father's departure an old wound was reopened. His description of this occasion is highly reminiscent of his description of the time when his father departed after leaving him at boarding school, when he was twelve years of age; the pain he felt was the same. He says, 'When I had seen father off at the station, and had looked after the train as long as it was in sight, even the smoke from it, and came home to my room and saw father's chair still standing near the little table on which the books and copybooks of the day before were still lying, though I know that we shall see each other again pretty soon, I cried like a child.' (118) Many years later he was to relive and express this feeling in his painting of Gauguin's empty chair, after the latter's departure from Arles where he had been living with Vincent for a short time.

As the time of the examinations gets closer Vincent's anxiety increases, 'for me things are becoming more and more serious as the examination draws nearer' (118), and 'it certainly is very doubtful that I shall ever succeed, I mean, shall ever pass all the examinations . . . There are so many, many things one has to know, and though they try to reassure me it constantly gives me a terribly anxious feeling'. (119) In the end Vincent gave up in his efforts. According to his teacher, Dr Mendes da Costa, Vincent, after a reasonably good start, was beaten by the Greek verbs. He would say, 'Mendes, do you seriously believe that such horrors are indispensable to a man who wants to do what I want to do: give peace to poor creatures and reconcile them to their existence here on earth?' (122a) He would have given up earlier but whenever he was discouraged he was asked again and again by the family to have another try. Mendes further remarks that Vincent was at the time in the habit of punishing himself whenever he felt he had neglected a duty. He did so by means of using a cudgel against his back and by lying on the floor of a little wooden shed, without bed or blanket, during the winter. He would not infrequently be without an overcoat in winter as another form of punishment. All this points to the strict nature of his conscience, the severity of his super-ego and his high ego ideals, as well as to a somewhat masochistic compliance on the part of his ego.

During all this time he drew occasionally, most often little illustrations to a Biblical subject, or maps of Palestine, of Paul's travels, etc.

Towards the end of the Amsterdam period Vincent frequented the house of his Uncle Cor (an art dealer too), where he admired many wood-drawings appearing in the magazine *L'Art*. He learned through his uncle of the death of the painter Daubigny. His reaction and comments show that deep in his unconscious he may be starting to consider art as a possible alternative for himself. They further show that even if this were to be the case, at this point in his development he could not allow himself any degree of originality but would have to be a follower. His father complex would force him to follow his own father's mediocre steps. His true creative freedom and originality are still some years away and hanging on the outcome of a number of developments still to take place. He writes to his brother 'the work of such men, if well understood, touches more deeply than one is aware. It must be good to die, conscious of having performed some real good and knowing that one will live through this work, at least in the memory of some'. (120) His submission to the dictates of his elders can be inferred from the following passage: 'Later, others – if there are any – can do no better than follow in the footsteps of such predecessors and do their work in the same way', a position that he strongly defended for some time during his first years as a painter, against the suggestions of Theo who was trying to interest him in the extremely original impressionist movement. Vincent for some time until he was able to free himself, was to defend the traditional forcefully.

ROULIN

e Postman at Arles though a modest and uneducated man took a great liking to Vincent
i was a constant source of support to the latter. It was he who took Vincent back to the
low House after the painter in a fit of madness had presented Rachel, the prostitute,
h his severed ear lobe. Vincent was a frequent visitor to the postman's house where he
s always received as a friend. In repayment he has immortalized in his portraits, not only
postman but his wife and children as well. The importance of this man's support and
ndship for Vincent can be seen in the fact that the postman's departure from Arles was
nediately followed by one of Vincent's mental breakdowns. (See Chapter 15, Vincent's
ntal Illness, page 119.)

7. THE GARDEN AT ST PAUL'S

Vincent spent many weeks as an inmate in this mental asylum the garden of which is represented here. In his lucid periods he was allowed to paint and many a canvas testifies to the life in the asylum. Others depict the views to be seen from his cell window at St Remy, where the hospital was located. In his disturbed periods he cried out incessantly, was deluded and hallucinated, with what he called perverted ideas about religion. Occasionally he had wanted to kill himself, eating his oil paints. (See Chapter 15, Vincent's Mental Illness, page 125.)

Photo by courtesy of the Kroller Müller Museum, Otterlo, Holland

❧ 6 ❧

VINCENT THE PREACHER
AND BUDDING PAINTER
The Etten-Borinage-Brussels Period:
July 1878 – April 1881

AFTER abandoning his studies in Amsterdam in July 1878 Vincent went to stay for a month with his parents at Etten. There he made a little drawing in pen, ink and pencil after E. Briton's 'A Sunday Morning'. In August he went to Taecken near Brussels to the training school for Evangelists where it was possible to qualify for a position after only three months.

Though it seems that Vincent arrived in Taecken by August 25th, there are no known letters to Theo until one written three months later on November 15th, when it seems that the two brothers spent the day together. More signs appear of an increasing competition between his religious call and painting, perhaps because he already foresaw another failure. He had been drawing and once included a sketch for Theo (Au Charbonnage) saying, 'I should like to begin making rough sketches of some of the many things that I meet on my way, but as it would probably keep me from my real work, it is better not to start'. (126) More and more art delineates itself as a possible substitute for religion and God, as a cure for his loneliness. *'How rich art is; if one can only remember what one has seen, one is never without food for thought or truly lonely, never alone.'* (126) By now the three months probation period was coming to an end but Vincent was not to be offered a position because he was lacking in discipline. This evidenced itself once during a Dutch grammar lesson. When asked a question, 'Van Gogh, is this the nominative or dative?' he answered, 'Oh sir, I really don't care.' (126a) The following incident belongs to this period too. During a French exercise the word *falaise* occurred and Vincent wanted to draw *une falaise* on the blackboard to illustrate its meaning, but the master considered it unnecessary. Once the lesson was finished and the master had gone, Vincent started to draw it on the blackboard. When somebody tugged at his jacket to make fun of him, Vincent turned around with an expression of rage on his face and gave his teaser a terrific blow. It was this type of incident that presumably disqualified him for work. A further reason for his failure was his inability to preach which forced him to read his sermons from a script – a surprising fact if we think of the marked ability to express himself shown in the letters. Though there are those who can express themselves well in writing but not in speaking, it seems possible that this inability was the result of the identification with his father. The latter was not good at preaching either and it may well have been that Vincent was under a compulsion not to surpass him.

Without the support of the evangelists and with the help of his father, Vincent went to the miner's district of the Borinage in Belgium where he lodged with a Mr van der Haegen.

He visited the sick, gave classes on the Bible and in the evenings gave lessons to his landlord's children. In January 1879 he was finally given a temporary position. It was a six month's trial period at Wasmes with a salary of 50 francs. Once there he gave away everything he had to the poor, the sick and the needy: his clothes, his shoes and even his bed. He moved into a simple wooden hut, sleeping on straw over the bare boards. The church authorities found his behaviour too good and too eccentric. They were alarmed at Vincent's disreputable looks which they thought diminished the dignity of his position. An old pastor who knew Vincent at this time said of him, 'His Dutch cleanliness was singularly abandoned, soap was banished as a wicked luxury – and when our evangelist was not wholly covered with a layer of coal dust, his face was usually dirtier than that of the miners. Exterior details did not trouble him.' (143a) The old pastor further remarked on Vincent's profound sensitivity which extended to all living creatures. He was told by the family with whom Vincent boarded that whenever Vincent found a caterpillar on the ground in the garden, he carefully picked it up and took it to a tree.

Vincent was reprimanded several times by the church authorities; his father tried to convince him of the need to compromise, to find a happy medium, but all to no avail. In the end he was dismissed from his position.

Curiously enough during all this time Vincent had in fact been drawing a great deal. He had always looked at nature and at objects with the eye of an artist. His descriptions, as later his paintings, were sketched quickly in a few traces, capable of conveying the whole story and of scoring the fullest impact. Thus for example he writes to his brother 'Most of the miners are thin and pale from fever; they look tired and emaciated, weatherbeaten and aged before their time. On the whole the women are faded and worn. Around the mine are poor miners' huts, a few dead trees black from smoke, thorn hedges, dunghills, ash dumps, heaps of useless coal, etc. Maris could make a wonderful picture of it.

'I will try to make a little sketch of it presently to give you an idea of how it looks.' (129)

He was finally dismissed from his position as an evangelist in July 1879. This new failure must be accounted for. His becoming a pastor had been a most cherished ideal for him for a long time and now that after many earlier failures and difficulties he had reached it, it is in many ways surprising to see that he set out to destroy the opportunity he had been given. He was given several warnings that his behaviour was unacceptable but he showed a complete inability to accept and to adapt himself to the conditions demanded by reality. Obviously many powerful unconscious forces which he was unable to handle forced him to behave in this self-destructive way, ignoring what was at stake for him.

He was dismissed largely because of his inability to compromise with the evangelists' authorities. They demanded some moderation in his extreme, charitable behaviour so as to keep the necessary respect for the dignity of the ecclesiastical position he held. A pastor dressed in rags, covered with dirt and sleeping on the floor of a hut was not their idea of a 'servant of God'. But Vincent was a man of strong passions and impulses and had singlemindedly established for himself the most difficult and high ideals conceivable. These ego ideals are best represented in a passage from Renan that he quoted to his brother in a letter from the London period: 'To act well in this world one must give up all selfish aims. The people who become the missionary of a religious thought, have no other fatherland than this thought. Man is not on this earth only to be happy, he is not only there to be simply honest, he is there to realize great things for humanity, to attain

51

nobility and to surpass the vulgarity in which the existence of almost all individuals drags on.' (26)

Vincent was already very disturbed and in the setting-up of such ideals and standards he was no doubt influenced by the fact that his father was a parson and that he idealized him as a model of perfection to follow. But this idealization, being his way of coping with very conflictive negative feelings towards his father carried with it the seeds of destruction. On the one hand he felt compelled to behave like this idealized figure, identifying with it, on the other hand, because of the negative feelings hidden behind this idealization and identification he was compelled to show his 'self-righteous pharisaic father' how a true christian ought to behave to his fellow human beings when at the service of God. Thus hidden under this extreme form of behaviour lay a most aggressive accusation of the consciously 'beloved' father.

Vincent, as pointed out by Dr Westerman Holstijn[1], had made an unconscious identification with Father-God-Christ and was in fact behaving accordingly. There are those who think that in his painting of the 'Pieta' he had substituted his own face for the Christ's.

Other factors played a similarly important role. There was for example his need to rebel against authority and his obstinacy, both possible results of the anal sadistic regression which led to his defiant attitude against established authority and conventions. Further his extreme kindness and pity was in part, the result of the transformation of similarly strong aggressive tendencies. It was not easy for him to abandon his charitable behaviour since he had found through it a suitable non-conflictive outlet for his aggression. No less conflictive, it may be argued, was his oedipal rivalry with his father and his unconscious phantasy of taking his father's place as a clergyman – in itself a legitimate aim were it not for the conflict introduced by the oedipal rivalry and hostility towards the father.

Under these conditions it is not all surprising that the whole schema collapsed in the end and in the way it did. Had he been successful in dealing with these conflicts we might never have known Van Gogh the painter who was to develop out of this failure. Obviously the criteria of success in terms of personality

[1] Westerman Holstijn, A. J., *The Psychological Development of Vincent Van Gogh*, Imago, 1924.

equilibrium, economics and conflicts is not always parallel to what may constitute a most desirable outcome in social, artistic or scientific terms.

He now took to drawing as an alternative and a compensation but there was no fixed aim, no plan, no purpose.

He tried to tempt Theo with some drawings to stay for a day or so with him when, on his way to Paris, his brother was to pass through the Borinage, 'I would have some drawings to show you, types from here; it wouldn't be worthwile for you to leave the train for those alone . . . Often I draw into the night, to keep some souvenir and strengthen the thoughts raised involuntarily by the aspect of things here.' (131) He mentions the Reverend Mr Pietersen who paints and has good ideas about art, and who has asked him for one of his sketches of a miner. He asks Theo to thank Tersteeg for the box of paints and sketch book the latter sent to him, 'that is half full already', and refers to his having bought another big sketchbook of old Dutch paper.

In the middle of October he writes to thank Theo for his visit. 'It was a long time since we had seen each other or written, as we used to do. Still, it is better to be friends than to be dead to each other.' (132)

Vincent was now facing yet another terrible failure. His inner conflicts and contradictory impulses, combined with unfavourable external circumstances, have once again defeated his best conscious intentions and ideals. It is not difficult to imagine the terrible situation, moral, physical and economical, in which he found himself. He had lost faith; he had no work, friends or even prospects. Comparatively little is known of this period. The letter he writes to his brother contains many beautiful passages. He acknowledges how much his relationship with Theo means to him, 'When I saw you again and walked with you, I had the same feeling which I used to have more than I do now – as if life were something good and precious which one must value – and I felt more cheerful and alive than I have for a long time, because gradually life has become less precious, much more unimportant and indifferent to me – at least, it seemed so. When one lives with others and is united by a feeling of affection, one is aware of a reason for living and perceives that one is not quite worthless and superfluous, but perhaps good for something: we need each other and make the same journey as travelling companions, but the feeling of proper self-esteem also depends very much on our relations with others . . . Like everyone else, I feel the need of family and friendship, of affection, of friendly intercourse; I am not made of stone or iron, like a hydrant or a lamp-post, so I cannot miss these things without being conscious of a void and feeling a lack of something, like any other intelligent and decent man. I tell you this to let you know how much good your visit had done me. And just as I hope that we two shall not be estranged from each other, I hope the same may be true in regard to all at home. But for the moment I do not feel very much like going back there, and I am strongly inclined to stay here. Perhaps the fault is mine, and you may be right that I do not see it clearly.' (132)

Theo and the family were distressed because of the lack of aim and purpose in Vincent's life at this point. Theo deeply offended his brother by saying to Vincent that he was afraid that he was too fond of spending his days in idleness and that it was time to end this and work. Vincent answered, 'You would also be mistaken if you thought that I would do well to follow your advice literally to become an engraver of bill headings and visiting cards, or a book-keeper or a carpenter's apprentice – or else to devote myself to being a baker – or many similar things (curiously different and hard to combine) that other people advise me.' (132) He continued, 'May I observe that this is rather strange sort of "idleness". It is somewhat difficult for me to defend myself, but I should be very sorry if, sooner or later, you could not see it differently – I am not sure it would be right to combat such an accusation by becoming a baker, for instance. It would indeed be a decisive answer (always supposing that it were possible to assume, quick as lightning, the form of a baker, a barber, or a librarian); but at the same time it would be a foolish answer, more or less like the action of the man who, when reproached with cruelty for riding a donkey, immediately dismounted and continued his way with the donkey on his shoulders.

'Now, all jesting aside, I really think it would be better if the relation between us became more friendly on both sides. If I had to believe that I were troublesome to you or to the people at home, or were in your way, of no good to anyone, and if I should be obliged to feel like an intruder or an outcast, so that I were better off dead, and if I should have to try to keep out of your way more and more – if I thought this were really the case, a feeling of anguish would overwhelm me, and I should have to struggle against despair. This is a thought I can hardly bear, and still harder to bear is the thought that so much discord, misery and trouble between us, and in our home, is caused by me. If it were indeed so, then I might wish that I had not much longer to live.' (132)

He ends the letter by telling his brother that he has drawn yet another portrait and that he will be very glad if he writes again soon. It is not known what Theo's answer to this letter was, if any. If there was an answer it cannot have been too positive because there is now an interruption of nine months in the correspondence between the brothers. The silence is broken 'somewhat reluctantly' by Vincent when Theo sends fifty francs to him through their parents, not directly. The letter is perhaps the most moving of all written by him. He says to his brother 'to a certain degree you have become a stranger to me, and I have become the same to you, more than you may think; perhaps it would be better for us not to continue in this way'. (133)

He has kept out of the way of the family as nine months earlier he said he would do if he felt he was troublesome to his brother or the others at home. He writes 'perhaps you know I am back in the Borinage. Father would rather I stay in the neighbourhood of Etten; I refused, and in this I think I acted for the best. Involuntarily, I have become more or less a kind of impossible and suspect personage in the family, at least somebody whom they do not trust, so how could I in any way be of any use to anybody? Therefore, above all, I think the best and most reasonable thing for me to do is to go away and keep at a convenient distance, so that I cease to exist for you all.

'As moulting time – when they change their feathers – is for birds, so adversity or misfortune is the difficult time for us human beings. One can stay in it – in that time of moulting – one can also emerge renewed; but anyhow it must not be done in public and it is not at all amusing, therefore the only thing to do is to hide oneself. Well, so be it.'

He expresses his wish for a reconciliation, 'Now, though it is very difficult, almost impossible, to regain the confidence of a whole family, which is not quite free from prejudices and other qualities as fashionable and honourable, I do not quite despair that by and by, slowly but surely, a cordial understanding may be renewed between some of us. And in the very first place, I should like to see that entente cordiale, not to put it stronger, re-established between Father and me; and I desire no less to see it re-established between us two. An entente cordiale is infinitely better than misunderstandings.'

He shows a great deal of insight into some of his difficulties. Unfortunately his awareness of such difficulties and their consequences does not help him to behave differently or to control himself any better, 'I am a man of passions, capable of and subject to doing more or less foolish things, which I happen to repent, more or less, afterwards. Now and then I speak and act too hastily, when it would have been better to wait patiently. I think other people sometimes make the same mistakes. Well, this being the case, what's to be done? Must I consider myself a dangerous man, incapable of anything? I don't think so. But the problem is to try every means to put those selfsame passions to good use.' He is still hurt by what his brother called his 'going down', his 'doing nothing'. It is important to notice that at this point he still has no definite aim of his own as to his future and though he reads and draws a certain amount he has not yet decided formally to become a painter. This step was in the end to be taken at Theo's suggestion and for the sake of the 'entente cordiale' with him. The letter continued 'Now for more than five years—I do not know exactly how long—I have been more or less without employment, wandering here and there. You say, Since a certain time you have gone down, you have deteriorated, you have not done anything, Is this quite true?

'It is true that occasionally I have earned my crust of bread, occasionally a friend has given it to me in charity. I have lived as I could, as luck would have it, haphazardly. It is true that I have lost the confidence of many; it is true that my financial affairs are in a sad state; it is true that the future is only too gloomy; it is true that I might have done better – it is true that I've lost time in terms of earning my bread; it is true that even my studies are in a rather sad and hopeless condition, and that my needs are greater – infinitely greater – than my possessions. But is this what you call "going down", is this what you call "doing nothing"?

'You will perhaps say, But why didn't you continue as they wanted you to – they wanted you to go through the university?

'My only answer is, the expenses were too heavy, and besides, that future was not much better than the one on the road now before me.

'But I must continue on the path I have taken now. If I don't do anything, if I don't study, if I don't go on seeking any longer, I am lost. Then woe is me. That is how I look at it: to continue, to continue, that is what is necessary.

'But you will ask, What is your definite aim?

'That aim becomes more definite, will stand out slowly and surely, as the rough draft becomes a sketch, and the sketch becomes a picture – little by little, by working seriously on it, by pondering over the idea, vague at first, over the thought that was fleeting and passing, till it gets fixed.'

He takes exception to his brother's saying that since they walked together years earlier, near the old canal and mill of Ryjswijk Vincent has changed so much that he is not the same any more. He responds 'Well, that is not quite true. What has changed is that my life then was less difficult and my future seemed less dark; but the inner state, my way of looking at things and my way of thinking, has not changed. If there has been any change at all, it is that I think and believe and love more seriously now what I already thought and believed and loved then.

'So you must not think that I disavow things – I am rather faithful in my unfaithfulness and, though changed, I am the same; my only anxiety is, How can I be of use in the world? Can't I serve some purpose and be of any good? How can I learn more and study certain subjects profoundly? You see, that is what pre-occupies me constantly; and then I feel imprisoned by poverty, excluded from participating in certain work, and certain neces-sities are beyond my reach.'

He comes back to the very painful point of his being an idler and writes what is perhaps one of the most beautiful passages in his letters as well as the best description of a neurotic inhibition of work of which I am aware: 'I write somewhat at random what-ever comes to my pen. I should be very glad if you could see in me something more than an idle fellow. Because there are two kinds of idleness, which are a great contrast to each other. There is the man who is idle from laziness and from lack of character, from the baseness of his nature. If you like, you may take me for such a one.

57

'On the other hand, there is the idle man who is idle in spite of himself, who is inwardly consumed by a great longing for action but does nothing, because it is impossible for him to do anything, because he seems to be imprisoned in some cage, because he does not possess what he needs to become productive, because circumstances bring him inevitably to that point. Such a man does not always know what he could do, but he instinctively feels, I am good for something, my life has a purpose after all, I know that I could be quite a different man! How can I be useful, of what service can I be? There is something inside of me, what can it be? This is quite a different kind of idle man; if you like, you may take me for such a one!

'A caged bird in spring knows quite well that he might serve some end; he is well aware that there is something for him to do, but he cannot do it. What is it? He does not quite remember. Then some vague ideas occur to him, and he says to himself, "The others build their nests and lay their eggs and bring up their little ones"; and he knocks his head against the bars of the cage. But the cage remains, and the bird is maddened by anguish.

' "Look at that lazy animal," says another bird passing, "he seems to be living at ease".'

'Yes, the prisoner lives, he does not die; there are no outward signs of what passes within him – his health is good, he is more or less gay when the sun shines. But then the season of migration comes, and attacks of melancholia – "But he has everything he wants," say the children that tend him in his cage. He looks through the bars at the overcast sky where a thunderstorm is gathering, and inwardly he rebels against his fate. "I am caged, I am caged, and you tell me I do not want anything, fools! You think I have everything I need! Oh! I beseech your liberty, that I may be a bird like other birds!"

'A certain idle man resembles this idle bird.

'And circumstances often prevent men from doing things, prisoners in I do not know what horrible, most horrible cage. There is also – I know it – the deliverance, the tardy deliverance. A justly or unjustly ruined reputation, poverty, unavoidable circumstances, adversity – that is what makes men prisoners.

'One cannot always tell what it is that keeps us shut in, confines us, seems to bury us; nevertheless, one feels certain barriers, certain gates, certain walls. Is all this imagination, fantasy? I don't think so. And one asks, "My God! is it for long, is it forever, is it for all eternity?"

'Do you know what frees one from this captivity? It is every deep, serious affection. Being friends, being brothers, love, that is what opens the prison by some supreme power, by some magic force. Without this, one remains in prison. Where sympathy is renewed, life is restored.

'And the prison is also called prejudice, misunderstanding, fatal ignorance of one thing or another, distrust, false shame. But I should be very glad if it were possible for you to see me as something more than an idle man of the worst type.' (133)

This letter leads to a reconciliation between the brothers. Vincent writes again very much as he has done before. There are for the moment no complaints or recriminations. In the letter that follows a month later Vincent is fully occupied drawing; he asks his brother to send prints for him to copy, for 'Les Travail des Champs', and to get Mr Tersteeg to send *Exercises au Fusain* by Barque (studies from the nude). He is thus undertaking seriously the study of drawing, and moving in the direction of becoming a painter. It seems that in doing so he is now following a suggestion of Theo's which had been made more than once in the past. That he does so as a means of reconciliation with Theo is made quite explicit: 'Well, these are the things I want to study. It is because I think you would rather see me doing some work than nothing that I write to you on this subject, and perhaps it might be a reason for restoring the *entente cordiale* and the sympathy between us, and make us of some use to one another.' (134) He further describes a drawing he has sketched 'representing miners, men and women, going to the shaft in the morning through the snow . . . passing shadows, dimly visible in the twilight' and includes a hasty sketch of it 'so you can see what it's like'. He asks for Theo's comments 'What do you think of the sketch – do you think the idea good?' (134)

In some respects this letter is a turning point. Vincent is now finally, after a long detour, on the road to painting. His development as a painter, as a creative painter, is still far from secure; a number of interesting developments in his personality must take place before he can get in touch with his enormous potential as a creative artist, before he can gain control and fully take command of it. But this special talent, this ego potential, is still to be awakened; it is by no means the only direction in which his personality is endowed with great potentialities; but it will be the one to develop further favoured by the vicissitudes of Vincent's conflicts and inner life and the chance environmental factors he had to contend with. As Elgar says, 'Vincent might just as easily have become a thinker, a poet, a hero or a saint as a painter. It may be thought, in fact, that he became all these at once',[1] A man is thus the final product of himself and of his circumstances.

The connection between his taking up drawing and his wish to restore his relationship with Theo is soon to disappear from his conscious awareness. A month later he is referring to his taking up drawing as something he has decided in his own right and independently of anything and anybody. It may be due to the fact that the connection brings about as well the painful realization of his dependence on his brother and that this must be obliterated from his consciousness, 'I cannot tell you how happy I am to have taken up drawing again. I had been thinking of it for a long time, but I always considered the thing impossible and beyond my reach' (136) and, 'Well, even in that deep misery I felt my energy revive, and I said to myself, In spite of everything I shall rise again: I will take up my pencil, which I have forsaken in my great discouragement, and I will go on with my drawing. From that moment everything has seemed transformed for me; and now I have started and my pencil has become somewhat docile, becoming more so every day.' (136) There is of course no question as to the fact that drawing is quickly becoming something in its own right whatever the original reasons for working at it seriously. It is indeed a very suitable sublimatory outlet bringing about important changes in Vincent's ego and personality.

He continues to study and after the *Exercises au Fusain* which he has been working on from early morning till night, he worked with the *Cours de Dessin Barque* and reads books on anatomy and perspective. 'Their style is very dry, and at times those books are terribly irritating, but still I think I do well to study them.' (136) All this time he tries his very best to comply with his brother, to be a good boy, 'I hope that you will not be too dissatisfied with the drawings after Millet when you see them.' (135) He is in a rage of work that for the moment is not producing brilliant results. He

[1] Elgar, Frank., *Van Gogh, A Study of his Life and Work*, Thames and Hudson, London.

says then 'But I hope these thorns will bear their white blossoms in due time, and that this apparently sterile struggle is no other than the labour of childbirth. First the pain, then the joy.' (136) This conscious comparison of his work with the labour of child-birth is to be repeated frequently later on in connection with the creation of his paintings. 'An artist's work and his private life are like a woman in childbirth and her baby. You may look at her child but you may not lift her chemise to see if it is blood-stained.' (181) It betrays his unconscious passive-feminine identifications; in this context the painting are the babies he produces for Theo and in collaboration with Theo who fecundates him (among other ways by sending him the money for his economic support). Theo is thus in Vincent's unconscious the father of these children and it is not surprising that when Theo is years later engaged and a child is born of this union, Vincent, though consciously happy, is, unconsciously, shattered. His babies are no longer enough for Theo.

At this point his father tells him that he will send sixty francs a month. This money is in fact being sent by Theo but Vincent does not yet know this.

In October he moves to Brussels and the possibility of entering L'Ecole de Beaux Arts there is considered. After some hesitation Vincent applies for admission. He is at the same time studying and drawing the human body.

Theo stops writing for several months. Vincent is annoyed and writes asking if Theo is not corresponding because of the fear that he may ask for money, 'if that is the reason for your silence, you might at least have awaited until I tried to squeeze something out of you, as the saying goes'. (139) He now wants to go to The Hague for some time and asks his brother if he knows of any reason not to go.

He is working from models almost every day, an old porter, working men, some boys. He writes 'I love landscape very much, but I love ten times more those studies from life'. (140)

In April 1881 Vincent learns that it is Theo who is supporting him economically. He thanks him while at the same time stating that living expenses are always at least a hundred francs a month, complaining about his two very rich uncles who do not help him in any way. He had quarrelled three years ago with one, C.M., and is hoping Theo will make things better betweeen them. Since there are economic difficulties, he suggests going to Etten (with his parents) as an alternative to The Hague. 'If you think right, you may write to Father about it. I am willing to give in about dress or anything else to suit them.' (142)

Around this time his mother wrote about him: 'I am always so afraid that wherever Vincent may be or whatever he may do, he will spoil everything by his eccentricity, his queer ideas and views of life.' His father added 'It grieves us so to see that he literally knows no joy of life, but always walks with bent head, whilst we did all in our power to bring him to an honourable position! It seems as if he deliberately chooses the most difficult path.'

Before leaving Brussels for Etten, as was finally decided, he requests the approval of his brother for the work he has been doing. Thus he continues to try to comply with and to please Theo with his work and drawings, just as earlier he tried equally hard to please his father.

'I am sending you three sketches which are clumsy as yet, but from which you will see, I hope, that I am gradually improving. You should take into account that it is only a short time since I started drawing, although I made little sketches when a boy. And that during this winter I thought it most important to make rigidly accurate anatomical studies, not my own compositions.' (143)

❧ 7 ❧

THE END OF THE RELIGIOUS PHASE
The Etten Period: April 1881 – December 1881

DURING this period there was an increasing deterioration of Vincent's relationship with his home and especially of the relationship with his father. The very old conflicts with his father, especially his hostility and negative feelings so far expressed covertly and strongly reacted against, were to find an increasingly overt form of expression. The previous idealization of the father was thus coming to an end, transforming itself, if anything, into a sort of 'negative idealization'. This transformation allowed Vincent to split his ambivalent feelings in such a way that the father became the recipient of most of his negative feelings and hostility which was thus largely directed away from Theo who had become in the meantime a father substitute for him and the recipient of his positive feelings.

This split of the ambivalent feelings between two father figures, a wholly and increasingly bad figure and a good one, helps to explain Vincent's very special relationship to his brother and its permanent character. As we will see, one of Vincent's main difficulties was his inability to relate to anybody, especially those in authority or above him for any length of time. Not that his relationship to Theo was always free of difficulties and negative feelings, far from it. But thanks partly to this split, partly to other factors, and perhaps especially because of Theo's infinite patience, it was at least a workable relationship, probably the only permanent and durable one of which Vincent was capable. We will come back to this point in the chapter 'On Further Comments on the Relationship to Theo and Others'. At Etten he continued his drawing and reading though the latter he perhaps did not do as much as during the Borinage period. He drew his sister Wilhelmien and a girl with a sewing machine and toys, with the idea of finding employment, 'if you should hear of a vacancy for a draftsman, think of me'. (144)

After spending some time at Etten he went for a trip to The Hague where he saw Tersteeg, Mauve (a well-established painter at the time, married to one of his cousins), and Bosboom. The last two particularly liked his drawing and gave him some technical hints. Mauve advised him to start painting immediately, but Vincent was to remain hesitant and reluctant about taking the step into colour for quite some time. His fear of failing, of not being able, held him back, 'Now and then I try water colour and sepias, but this does not succeed immediately.' (152) He knows, he feels, that there is something special about his drawing that must not be lost in his paintings. He states, 'Painting is drawing at the same time' (152), but he will not be able to realize this formula fully until a few years later with the final realization of his unique and personal style, which combines to perfection the colourist and the draftsman. His paintings thus finally become in some ways like beautiful drawings in colour.

It is at this time as Vincent finds it more and more difficult to relate to people and grows more and more isolated from human relationships that he turns instead to nature that 'talks to him with a thousand voices' as his sister was to say. In this respect trees are especially representative and symbolic. He is of course extremely interested in drawing the figure, in drawing from the model and it is clear that this is very much determined by the opportunity it gives him of a human relationship for which he is always longing, that it is a break from his constant and painful loneliness. For as long as the model is there and he has company he is alive, he is not alone. He refers to Corot's love of the figure and to how he 'drew and modelled every trunk with the same devotion and love as if it were a figure', (149) and 'If one draws a willow as if it were a living being – and after all, it really is – then the surroundings follow in due course if one has concentrated all one's attention only on that same tree, not giving up until one has put some life into it.' (152) In one of the letters he sends to his brother from the asylum at St Remy towards the end of his life the following description of one of the paintings of the garden there appears. 'The nearest tree is merely a large trunk which has

he 'house of friends' where Vincent dreamt of establishing a community of
.ffering fellow painters living under the same roof with Gauguin as their
bbot. Here he lived with Gauguin for a short period and suffered his first
ental breakdown. Through these windows he was mocked at by the citizens
" Arles who persecuted him and wanted him banned from the house and the
ty as a public danger. Here he painted with candles all over his hat to illuminate
s canvases. (See Chapter 13, The Yellow House, page 106 and Chapter 16,
he Two Empty Chairs, page 134.)
hoto by courtesy of the Amsterdam Municipal Museum

The ascetic quality of his room as depicted here contrasts sharply with the meticulous arrangement of Gauguin's room at Arles (c.f. the picture of Gauguin's armchair and its background. See too Chapter 16, pages 134–5 for a description of the extreme care Vincent took in preparing Gauguin's room before the latter's arrival at Arles). It was presumably in this room, perhaps in front of this mirror, that Vincent mutilated his ear lobe. It was here that he was found by Gauguin and the police in a state of near unconsciousness after having bled profusely. (See Chapter 16, The Two Empty Chairs, page 136.)

Photo by courtesy of the Amsterdam Municipal Museum

been struck by lightning and then sawn off. But a side branch shoots up very high and then tumbles down in an avalanche of dark green pine needles. This sombre giant, proud in his distress, is contrasted – to treat them as living beings – with the pallid smile of a last rose of the fading bush opposite him . . . you will realize that this combination of red ochre, green saddened by grey, and the use of heavy black outlines produces something of the sensation of anguish, the so-called *noire-rouge*, from which certain of my companions in misfortune frequently suffer. Moreover the effect of the great tree struck down by lightning and the sickly greeny pink smile of the last flower of autumn merely serve to heighten this idea.' Is it not legitimate to ask if Vincent did not see himself in this tree? The strong link in his mind between human beings and nature in general is perhaps best described in the following passage: 'In all nature, for instance in trees, I see expression and soul, so to speak. A row of pollard willows sometimes resembles a procession of almshouse men. Young corn has something inexpressibly pure and tender about it, which awakens the same emotion as the expression of a sleeping baby, for instance.

'The trodden grass at the roadside looks tired and dusty like the people of the slums. A few days ago, when it had been snowing, I saw a group of savoy cabbages standing frozen and benumbed, and it reminded me of a group of women in their thin petticoats and old shawls which I had seen standing in a little hot-water-and-coal shop early in the morning.' (242)

The drama of his relationship to his father and mother was to unfold itself around his falling in love with his cousin Kee. Kee, it will be remembered, was the daughter of the Reverend Mr Stricker. Vincent had met her and her husband, in Amsterdam. Now, recently widowed, she had come in mourning to Etten. After a few weeks Vincent declared his love. Kee rejected him in no uncertain terms, but he was not easily going to take no for an answer. He thought that if he was given time and the opportunity to see her, she might change her 'no, never, never'. He wrote to Theo, 'Old boy, for the present I look upon that "no, never, never" as a block of ice which I press to my heart to thaw.' (154) He was convinced for no reason at all that his greatest difficulties were with the older people, his parents, Uncle Stricker, etc., 'who consider the question settled and done with, and will try to force me to give up'. (154) 'So do not accuse me of disrespect toward the older people. I only believe that they are decidedly *against* it; they will take care that Kee and I cannot see each other or speak to each other or write to each other because they know perfectly well that if we saw each other or wrote to each other or spoke to each other, there would be a chance of Kee changing her mind . . . The older people will change in this affair, not when Kee changes her mind, but only when I have become somebody who earns at least 1,000 guilders a year.' (153)

Vincent was now irritated because Theo did not support him openly, and in what follows we see not only the crumbling of the idealization of his mother and father, but also the verbalization (for the first time in his letters) of his awareness that Theo was a favoured sibling, that he was first in the parents' affection. 'Father and Mother are very good at heart but have little understanding of our inner feelings, and as little comprehension of your real circumstances as of mine. They love us with all their hearts – you especially – and we both, I as you, love them very much indeed; but alas, in many cases they cannot give us practical advice, and there are times when, with the best of intentions, they do not understand us. It is not our fault or theirs, but the difference in age and the difference in opinion and the difference in circumstances.' (155) He wanted Theo to intercede with his parents. 'A word from you perhaps influences them more than anything I can say, and it would be so much better, for them as well as for me, to let me go my way quietly.' (155) He argued with Theo, who wrote to him that home was and would remain their resting place come what may, and that Vincent should appreciate and respect this. Vincent answered, 'there is a resting place better, more necessary, more indispensable than our home with our parents, however good, however necessary, however indispensable it may be – and that is our own hearth and home, with our respective "she, and no other".

'There you are, oh man of business, closing profitable deals, your biggest deal – your own home with your own "she and no other".' (155)

He grew very resentful of his parents who had referred to his declaration of love to the only recently widowed Kee as 'untimely and indelicate', and who later accused him of 'breaking family ties'. He believed that while a word from his mother would have helped him greatly she not only refused to help but cut off every opportunity for him, 'she came to me with a face full of pity and with many comforting words, and I am sure she had prayed a beautiful prayer for me, that I might receive strength for resignation . . . But . . . that prayer has found no hearing, I have received strength for action'. (155)

Vincent wanted to make his drawings saleable because he needed money to visit Kee in Amsterdam in spite of all opposition and of Kee's refusal to have anything to do with him. He went on writing letters that remained unanswered by either Kee or her parents. When his family again mentioned his 'breaking family ties', he decided not to speak a word or to take any notice of his parents for several days, 'to make them feel how it would be if those family ties were really severed'. (158) His parents were astonished at this behaviour and the result was 'that Father grew very angry, ordered me out of the room with a curse, at least it sounded exactly like one! Father is used to having everyone give in to him when he's in a passion, even I, but this time I was quite determined to let him rage for once. In anger Father also said something like I had better leave the house and go elsewhere; but because it was said in a passion, I do not attach much importance to it.

'I have my models and my studio here; living elsewhere would be more expensive, and my work more difficult, and the models would cost more. But if Father and Mother said go in earnest to me, of course I should go. There are things which a man cannot put up with.' (158)

He continued: 'Of course I have also told Father and Mother a thing or two, for instance that they were very much in error on the subject of this love affair and that their hearts were hardened, and that they were completely closed to a more gentle and humane way of thinking. In short, that their way of thinking seemed narrow-minded to me – neither tolerant nor generous enough; and also that to me God would merely be an empty sound if one were forced to hide one's love and were not allowed to obey the heart's dictates.

'Well, I am quite willing to believe that at times I have not been able to curb my indignation when I heard "indelicate" and "breaking ties", but who could remain calm under it if there were no end to it?' (158)

The arguments between his father and Vincent grew stronger

and more bitter. At the same time Vincent was extremely hurt because the father was quite prepared to have him out of the house. He wrote, 'Besides, the disagreement between Father and Mother and myself is not so terrible, is not of such a nature that we could not stay together. But Father and Mother are getting old, and they have prejudices and old-fashioned ideas which neither you nor I can share any more. When Father sees me with a French book by Michelet or Victor Hugo, he thinks of thieves and murderers, or of "immorality"; but it is too ridiculous, and of course I don't let myself be disturbed by such opinions. So often I have said to Father, Then just read it, even a few pages of such a book, and you will be impressed yourself; but Father obstinately refuses. Just now, when this love took root in my heart, I re-read Michlet's book *L'Amour et La Femme*, and so many things became clear to me that would otherwise have been in riddles. I told Father frankly that under the circumstances I attached more value to Michelet's advice than to his own, if I had to choose which of the two I should follow.

'But then they bring up a story of a great uncle who was infected with French ideas and took to drink, and so they insinuate that I shall do the same. *Quelle misere !*' (159) And 'For heaven's sake, let them give in for once; it would be too foolish for a young man to sacrifice his energy to the prejudices of an old man.' (159)

Theo, at Vincent's insistence, tried to pour oil on these turbulent waters and wrote to his parents. He even sent money for the railway fare in case Vincent decided to go to Amsterdam to talk to Kee. His sister Wilhelmien was meantime checking to tell him when Kee would be back in Amsterdam. Vincent talked now of old grievances as well, 'Don't think that the recent regrettable scene was caused only by hot temper. Alas, previously when I declared that I would not continue my study in Amsterdam, and later in the Borinage when I refused to do what the clergymen wanted me to do, Father said something similar. So there is indeed a lasting, deep-rooted misunderstanding between Father and myself. And I believe that it never can be quite cleared up. But on both sides we can respect each other because we agree in so many things, though sometimes we have quite different – aye, even opposite – views.

'So I do not consider Father an enemy, but a friend who would be even more my friend if he were less afraid that I might "infect" him with French "errors" (?) I think if Father understood my real intentions, I could often be of some use to him, even with his sermons, because I sometimes see a text in quite a different light. But Father thinks my opinion entirely wrong, considers it contraband and systematically rejects it.' (161) Sometime later he will complain 'Just think, Theo, how different things might have been at home, for instance, if Father could have been less distrustful of me, a bit less suspicious; if, instead of considering me a person who could only do wrong, he had shown more patience and goodwill in order to understand my real intentions – in which he has always been sorely mistaken. In the first place, he would have felt less grief on my account, and would have been easier in his mind about me; and in the second place, he would have spared me much sorrow. For it is great sorrow to think, This is worse than having no home at all, no father, no mother, no relations – and I have often thought so, as I do now.' (201)

In December 1881 Vincent went back to The Hague, to the painter Mauve, for help and advice. He hoped to be there for a month or so. At the same time he paid short visits to Amsterdam, still determined to see and talk to Kee. This led to unpleasant and difficult scenes with the Reverend Mr Stricker and his wife. After one of many such scenes he 'felt chilled through and through to the depth of my soul . . . I did not want to be stunned by that feeling. Then I thought, I should like to be with a woman – I cannot live without love, without a woman'. (164) He thought this wish conflictive with his love for Kee but concluded 'whether I act rightly or wrongly, I cannot do otherwise . . . I need a woman, I cannot, I may not, I will not live without love. I am a man and a man with passions; I must go to a woman, otherwise I shall freeze or turn to stone – or in short, shall be stunned'. (164) He continued, 'Under the circumstances I fought a great battle within myself, and in the battle some things remained victorious, things which I knew of physic and hygienics and had learned by bitter experience. One cannot live too long without a woman with impunity . . . in short I came to the conclusion, I must see whether I can find a woman. And, dear me, I hadn't far to look. I found a woman, not young, not beautiful, rather tall and strongly built; she did not have a lady's hands like Kee, but the hands of one who works much; but she was not coarse or common, and had something very womanly about her.

'That woman has not cheated me – oh, he who regards all such women as cheats, how wrong he is, and how little understanding he shows. That woman was very good to me, very good, very kind – in what way I shall not tell my brother Theo, because I suspect my brother Theo of having had some such experience. So much the better for him.' (164)

He continued, 'Clergymen call us sinners, conceived and born in sin, bah! What dreadful nonsense that is. Is it a sin to love, to need love, not to be able to live without love ? I think a life without love a sinful and immoral condition.' (164)

Vincent had a long-standing interest in prostitutes with whose misery and unhappiness he could readily and easily identify. For the same reason he was always deeply moved in the presence of the poor, the peasant, the miner, in short in the presence of all those less favoured by life and fortune. He was himself, in his unconscious phantasies, one of them. We will see later that he considered himself the dog in his family. He explains, 'It is not just recently that I have had a heart for those women who are condemned and damned by the clergymen, the feeling is even older than my love for Kee. Often when I walked the streets quite lonely and forlorn, half ill and in misery, without money in my pocket, I looked after them and envied the men who could go with them, and felt as if those poor girls were my sister, in circumstances and experience. And, you see, it is an old feeling of mine, and is deeply rooted. Even as a boy I often looked up with infinite sympathy, with respect even, into a half-faded woman's face on which was written, as it were, Life in its reality has left its mark here.' (164)

Thus, not far from his twenty-ninth birthday, Vincent has what may well have been his first sexual experience with a woman, a prostitute. He is soon afterwards to settle down to live with her in spite of the opposition this arouses from all quarters.

With Mauve he paints a few studies and a few water colours, 'At all events, Theo, through Mauve I have got some insight into the mysteries of the palette and of water colouring.' (163) He is forced to spend more money than he ought to because of the woman and his family and this leads to further difficulties between him and his father. He wants Theo to send him some extra money. Towards the end of December he is back at Etten. He has for the time being idealized Mauve who becomes a semi-God, 'I do not wish to associate much with other painters. Each day I find Mauve cleverer and more trustworthy, and what more can I want?' (167) As usual this idealization will not last for very long. Vincent ends by irritating Mauve, quarrelling with him and provoking his ill will. Vincent's anal tendencies greatly irritated Mauve especially his dirty appearance and frequent habit of using his fingers to touch the canvas. He is quoted as having snapped at Mauve in a temper, 'What the hell does it matter, even if I did it with my heels, as long as it is good and has the right effect.' (435C)

HIS ASSOCIATION WITH CHRISTINE
(THE PROSTITUTE) AND HER CHILDREN
The Hague Period: December 1881 – September 1883

ON Christmas Day 1881 at Etten things came to a head between Vincent and his father. They had a violent scene that went so far that his father asked him to leave the house. Vincent left the same day and moved to The Hague.

Vincent explained that the argument was aroused through his refusal to go to church regularly which could not have failed to irritate his father, being as he was the village parson. He thought there were other reasons as well especially the love affair with his cousin Kee.

'I do not remember ever having been in such a rage in my life. I frankly said that I thought their whole system of religion horrible, and just because I had gone too deeply into those questions during a miserable period of my life I did not want to think of them any more, and must keep clear of them as of something fatal . . . Was I too angry, too violent? May be – but even so, it is settled now once and for all.' (166)

Theo wrote reproaching Vincent for his behaviour towards his father and Vincent replied on the same sheet of paper that Theo had written on. He was bitter and fought back point by point: 'The expression that it is my purpose to *embitter and spoil Father's and Mother's life* is in reality not your own; I know it, and have for a long time, as a Jesuitism of Pa's; and I have told Father, and Mother too, that I considered it a Jesuitism, and that it did not worry me in the slightest. Every time you say something to Father which he hasn't an answer for, he produces an expression of this kind; for instance, he will say, "You are murdering me," meanwhile reading the paper and smoking his pipe in complete tranquillity. So I take such expressions for what they really are.

'Or else Father will fly into a frightful rage, and as he is accustomed to people being scared of him under such circumstances, Father is surprised if somebody does not give way to his anger . . .

'If this last row had been an isolated case, things would have been different; but it was preceded by many rows, in the course of which, in a more quiet but resolute manner, I told Father a good many things which his Honour saw fit to fling to the winds. So as to the things I said when I lost my temper, I think the same when in a calmer mood, only for diplomatic reasons I am silent or express myself in other terms. But when I flew into a rage, my diplomacy was swept away, and, well, on this occasion I really let fly. I will not apologize for this, and as long as Father and Mother persevere in this mood, I shall not take anything back. Should they make up their minds to be more humane, more delicate of feeling and more honest, then I shall be glad to take everything back. But I doubt whether this will happen . . .

'That I shall regret it, etc. Before things reached the point they have come to now, I had many regrets and much grief, and I was sorely worried because there was so much hard feeling between Father and Mother, and myself. But now that things have gone so far, well so be it; and, to tell you the honest truth, I have no regrets any more, but involuntarily a feeling of deliverance. Should I later conclude that I did wrong, then I shall regret it, of course, but so far I have been unable to see how I could possibly have acted differently. When somebody says deliberately and resolutely to me, "Get out of my house, the sooner the better, and rather in half an hour than an hour," Well, my dear fellow, it won't be a matter of an hour before I shall be gone, and I shall never return, either. It was too bad. For financial reasons, and in order not to cause you more trouble, I should not have left of my own accord on insufficient grounds – this you must understand; but now that the "Get out" is not on my side but on theirs, my road is indicated clearly enough . . .

'I am not Father's enemy if I tell him some home truths occasionally – not even when I used some salty language in a fit of rage. Only it didn't help me, and Pa took offence. In case Pa alluded to my saying that the morality and religious system of ordained clergymen are not worth a fig to me since I have come to know so much of the *dessous des cartes*, I decidedly will not take this back, for I really mean it. However, when I am in a quiet mood, I don't speak of it; but when they want to force me to go to church or attach value to doing so, it is only natural that I tell them, This is out of the question.' (169)

His relationship to Mauve and Tersteeg once he was at The Hague remains good only for a short period of time. He would soon say of Mauve, 'It is not always easy for me to get on with Mauve or vice versa'. (173)

There were any number of reasons for the deterioration of these relationships but Vincent's association with Christine (Sien), the prostitute, whom he had taken into his house and even planned to marry was the final blow to them. There was also Vincent's neglect of his appearance, his shabby and dirty clothes, his obstinacy, his off-hand manner, his economic difficulties that sometimes forced him to importune his friends and so on.

He did not tell Theo about his association with Christine for quite some time. Meanwhile he was always complaining to Theo that the money he was sending (100 francs) was not enough, and asking for more for a multiplicity of reasons. He was really finding it very difficult to make ends meet since he had now responsibility for Christine, her child and even her mother. He complained to Theo who was unaware of the facts 'As you can imagine I am very hard pressed for money . . . I work as much as I can, but don't forget that I shall break down if I have too many cares and anxieties' (176) . . . 'If you can, send me the money for this month soon. I am making progress with my work, but cannot work without or with too little.' (179) . . . 'Can you send me some money soon?' (183). Such requests were in fact interminable.

As time went by he became somewhat paranoid in relation to Tersteeg whom he suspected of knowing about Christine and who, he feared, might tell Theo. If Theo delayed either to write or to send the money he grew very worried in case Tersteeg had turned Theo against him, 'Is it possible that you have heard something from Tersteeg that has influenced you?' (175) Similarly he was inclined to think that Mauve might have turned against him because of Tersteeg. In this respect he wrote to Theo 'Because Tersteeg poisoned Mauve's ear by saying, "Be careful, you can't trust him with money. Let him go, don't help him any longer; as a dealer I see no good coming of it" – or at least something like this.' (191) He continued: 'And when I said to him, Tersteeg, take it easy with that slander of yours, he looked astonished, he hadn't said a thing; he pretended I had only imagined it. Until one fine day he threatened me, "Mauve and I will see to it that you don't receive any more money from Theo". Then I no longer doubted, but realized he was betraying me.' (191)

Vincent was almost completely blind to the social implications of his living with Christine and the unavoidable repercussions of his behaviour in terms of his relationship to Mauve and Tersteeg.

At this stage it is convenient to examine the multiplicity of factors involved in his relationship to Christine.

First, Vincent had identified Christine with their old nurse at Zundert, Leen Vierman. He said, 'If my memory does not deceive me Sien is that kind of person'. (201) Unfortunately nothing is known about this or the importance and significance of this identification. Second, we should remember that Vincent was himself identifying unconsciously with the parson of Elliot's *Clerical Scenes* in the rescue of a prostitute, as we have pointed out earlier. Third, there was the role played by an identification with Theo, who in the past had a similar love affair with a 'woman of the people'. Unfortunately this cannot be properly assessed either for lack of sufficient information but Vincent will occasionally refer to this incident (see Letter 208). Fourth, we have to consider that the relationship to Christine started as a reaction to the disappointment of Vincent's love for his cousin Kee. He was frustrated and embittered not only with Kee but with her parents as well as with his own parents. He thought that they did not consider him good enough for her; that they objected because he was rough, peculiar and did not earn enough, he had no present and no future, etc. If not consciously at least unconsciously his relationship to Christine must have been his way of paying all of them back: They would come to regret 'obstructing' his relationship to Kee. There was as well the fact that he was at this point in his life under great pressure from his sexual instincts, as we have seen before, partly because of the breaking down of religious sublimations and restrictions. Thus he was to write later on hearing that Theo is not well, 'I tell you frankly that in my opinion one must not hesitate to go to a prostitute occasionally if there is one you can trust and feel something for, as there

75

really are many. For one who has a strenuous life it is necessary, in order to keep sane and well. One must not exaggerate such things and fall into excesses, but nature has fixed laws which it is fatal to struggle against . . . Well, you yourself know all you have to know on that subject. It would be well for you, it would be well for me, if we were married – but what can we do?' (173)

He now longed for a close relationship to a woman, for a feeling of being loved, and because of this need he was to blind himself for many months to reality factors in relation to Christine and her relationship to him. Following his usual pattern, Christine became very much idealized and even the shortcomings which he acknowledged in her were turned into assets in terms of their relationship. Finally he felt or deceived himself into believing that he was loved; that love had to be defended. He wrote later on, after having informed his brother, 'She said to me, "I know that you haven't much money, but even if you had less, I would put up with everything if only you stay with me and let me stay with you; I am so attached to you that I could not be alone again."

'If someone says that to me, and shows by everything – in deeds more than in words – that she means it, then no wonder that with her I drop the mask of reserve, almost of roughness, which I have worn so long because I did not want to flatter . . .

'Perhaps I can understand her better than anyone else because she has a few peculiarities which would have been repulsive to many others. First her speech which is very ugly and is a result of her illness; then her temper, caused by a nervous disposition, so that she has fits of anger which would be unbearable to most people.

'I understand these things, they don't bother me, and until now I have been able to manage them. On her side she understands my own temper, and it is sort of a tacit understanding between us not to find fault with each other.' (194)

Whatever one may conclude about this relationship it still remains that it is the closest to a home life, to a family of his own – for which he so longed all his life – that Vincent ever got.

Furthermore there is the fact that the massive anal regression that had taken place in his personality made the relationship to a prostitute a particularly suitable form of object choice, allowing for the gratification of important unconscious elements and phantasies belonging to the anal stage of development, a stage that played such a significant role in Vincent's character structure. In addition this relationship was, in terms of his anal regression, an aggressive, obstinate and provocative piece of behaviour.

Vincent's masochistic needs, unconscious guilt and need for punishment found an excellent opportunity of fulfilment in a relationship that was bound to bring much disapproval, rejection, isolation, suffering and difficulty into his life. Mr Tersteeg described this aspect accurately when he said to Vincent that he was 'just as foolish as a man who wanted to drown himself.' (216)

His uncle, C.M. the art dealer, with whom he had quarrelled years earlier came to see him and ordered a dozen drawings from him. Vincent was extremely happy, '*Theo, it is almost miraculous*!!!' (180) but when C.M. did not pay by return post Vincent complained: 'The drawings were certainly no worse than the specimen which he saw, and I had trouble enough making them, perhaps more than thirty guilders' worth. If people understood that nothing is nothing, and that days without a penny in my pocket are very hard and difficult, I think they would not begrudge me the little money I get from you which keeps me afloat in these hard times, nor unnerve me by reproaches for taking it from you.

'Don't I deserve my bread if I work hard? Or am I not worthy of the means which enable me to work? I only wish, brother, that you would come here soon and see for yourself whether I'm cheating you or not.' (183)

Suddenly and for no obvious reason, from Letter 181 onwards Vincent hardly ever again bothered to write the date on his letters as he had previously been in the habit of doing.

After months of hiding his association with Christine from his brother he felt forced to tell Theo about it. This he did in Letter 192 because of his fear at this moment that Mauve or Tersteeg might write to Theo. He had met Mauve and had asked him to come and see his work and talk things over. Mauve refused saying, 'I will certainly not come to see you, that's all over', adding 'you have a vicious character'. (192) Mauve's reaction was presumably largely due to Vincent's association with Christine. Vincent complained to his brother, 'They suspect me of something – it is in the air – I am keeping something back. Vincent is hiding something that cannot stand the light.

'Well gentlemen, I will tell you, you who prize good manners and culture, and rightly so if only be the true kind: which is the more delicate, refined, manly –to desert a woman or to stand by a forsaken woman?' (192)

He explained to Theo how he met this pregnant prostitute and took her for a model, 'Thank God, so far I have been able to protect her and her child [Christine, as well as being pregnant, had a daughter] from hunger and cold by sharing my own bread with her.' (192) The pregnant prostitute was ill and in need of help, and this as usual attracted his attention. 'The woman is now attached to me like a tame dove. For my part, I am only to marry once, and how can I do better than marry her? It is the only way to help her; otherwise misery would force her back into her old ways, which ends in a precipice.' (192) He closed this letter by saying, 'I had not forgotten another woman for whom my heart was beating, but she was far away and refused to see me; and this one walked the street in winter, sick, pregnant, hungry – I couldn't do otherwise, Mauve, Theo, Tersteeg, you have my bread in your hands, will you take it from me, or turn your back on me? Now I have spoken, and wait what ever will be said to me next.' (192)

Theo, once informed, asked Vincent to leave this woman but Vincent refused to do so, though he had no source of income to support her other than the money Theo sent him monthly. He argued, 'At present money is what the right of the strongest used to be. To contradict a person is fatal' (193), and 'being so, I risk my head when I contradict you but, Theo, I don't know I could do otherwise; if my head must be cut off, here is my neck. You know the circumstances and know that my life or death depends on your help. But I am between two fires. If I reply to your letter: Yes, Theo, you are right, I will give up Christine, then first I tell a lie in agreeing with you and second, I commit myself to doing a vile thing. If I contradict you and you act like T. and M., it will cost me my head, so to speak.

'Well, for heaven's sake, off with my head, if that's the way it has to be. The other thing is even worse.' (193)

Theo, though unhappy about Vincent's relationship to Christine, did not withdraw his help and concentrated on trying to disuade him from marrying her.

The rest of the family did not yet know of the relationship and Vincent begged Theo not to mention it to Uncle Vincent whom he was to see soon. 'They would consider it "immoral" or even worse.' Meanwhile he had received a kind letter from his father and mother that pleased him, but he wondered what would happen when they learnt about the affair with Christine and whether they would still speak kindly then.

Theo mentioned the possibility that if the family were informed they might want to take active steps against him such as declaring him incapable of dealing with his affairs and placing him under guardianship. To this Vincent reacted violently, writing:

'When you say, 'Only a few witnesses (and even false ones) would have to declare that you are unable to manage your own financial affairs; this would be sufficient to entitle Father to take away your civil rights and put you under guardianship" – if, I say, you really mean this, and think that particularly nowadays this might be an easy thing to do, I take the liberty to doubt it.' (204)

He warned Theo that he was not going to take this quietly and quoted a case he knew of somebody placed under guardianship by evil means against his will, who 'knocked his keeper's brains out with a poker'; when the case was investigated the man was acquitted. He continued, 'If you ask me, I do not think the family would do a thing like that, but you may counter that in the matter of the Gheel Asylum, they already tried. Alas, yes – Father is capable of it – but I tell you, if he dares attempt anything of the sort, I shall fight him to the limit. Let him think twice before he attacks me but once again I doubt whether they will have the courage to do it.' (204)

In successive letters Theo tells him quite frankly that he is being fooled by Christine but Vincent rejects such comments outright.

Vincent has soon to go to hospital where he will have to remain for a few weeks. He feels weak and unwell, and has been eating rather badly because of lack of means, but the main trouble is that Christine has given him some disease, presumably a gonorrhoea.

While Vincent is at the hospital, Christine has to go to Leyden for her confinement. Vincent claims that he is glad to be at the hospital because he hopes to get a statement from his doctor 'to the effect that I am not the person to be sent to Gheel [a mental institution] or to be put under guardianship.' (207)

While he was at the hospital his father came to visit him but Vincent kept silent about Christine.

He started to grow anxious about Christine while still at the hospital and finally went to Leyden to visit her, accompanied by Christine's mother and daughter. Christine had given birth in the meantime to a baby boy and Vincent was relieved that everything was finally all right. He immediately rented a larger and more expensive house in order to prepare a new home for Christine and the baby. A few weeks later there was another scene with Tersteeg who came to visit him and found the child and Christine still living in the house. He wrote: 'Never has a doctor told me that there was something abnormal about me in the way and in the sense Tersteeg dared to tell me this morning. That I was not able to think or that my mind was deranged. No doctor has told me this, neither in the past nor in the present; certainly I have a nervous constitution, but there is definitely no real harm in that. So those were serious insults on Tersteeg's part, just as they were on Pa's, but even worse, when he wanted to send me to Gheel. I cannot take such things lying down.' (216) The role that these threats of taking away his civil rights and sending him to a mental institution may well have played in his later and more serious nervous breakdowns and periods of incarceration in mental institutions will be discussed later.

He continued pleading with Theo not to withdraw his support in spite of the general opposition to his plans to marry Christine. He said, 'I know how only a short time ago I came home to a house that was not a real home with all the emotions connected with it now, where two great voids stared at me night and day. There was no wife, there was no child. I do not think there were fewer cares for all that, but certainly there was less love. And those two voids accompanied me, one on either side, in the street and at work, everywhere and always.

'There was no wife, there was no child.

'See, I do not know whether you have had that feeling which forces a groan or a sigh from us at moments when we are alone: My God, where is my wife: my God, where is my child? Is living alone worth while?' (213)

Under pressure he finally agreed to postpone the marriage indefinitely, so as to compromise with Theo, at least until such time as his 'drawing had progressed so far that I am independent'. He hoped to show Theo that he did not want to have his own way always and in everything and 'that I am willing to give in to your wishes as far as I can.' (217)

He continued to hope that in a few years, or even at present 'you will see things by me which will give you some satisfaction for your sacrifices'. (218) By this time some signs appeared of his being psychologically able to take an independent artistic position, in sharp contrast to his earlier attitudes and views where he had stated that the younger generation of artists could do nothing better than to follow closely on the paths indicated by their elders. Now he said, 'Personally I find in many modern pictures a peculiar charm which the old masters do not have . . . So, I think it was a mistake a few years ago when modern painters went through a period of imitating the old masters.' (218)

Theo was coming to The Hague and was going to use the opportunity to visit Vincent. Vincent remarked that he would want to see as much as possible of Theo but that it would be better if he did not accompany his brother in his visits to Mauve, Tersteeg, etc., giving his clothes as an excuse. He said 'I am so used to my working clothes, in which I can lie or sit on the sand or the grass, whichever is necessary (for in the country I never use a chair, only an old fish basket sometimes); so my dress is a little too Robinson Crusoe-like for paying calls with you.' (220)

Theo had been trying to get Vincent to do some more actual painting, water colours and oils, but Vincent remained hesitant and just wanted to go on drawing. 'I do not object to doing water colours; but their foundation is the drawing and then many other branches sprout from the drawing besides the water colour.' (221) He reasoned that he stuck to his drawing firstly because he wants a firmer hand in drawing and secondly because oils and water colours were so much more expensive. Deep within him his fear of changing from drawing to painting (he had been drawing consistently now for two whole years) was due partly to a fear of failing, to the fear of not being successful at painting. He wrote, 'I restrained myself up to now [in regard to painting] and stuck to drawing just because I know so many sad stories of people who threw themselves headlong into painting – who sought the solution of their problems in technique and awoke disillusioned, without having made any progress, but having become up to their ears in debt because of the expensive things they had spoiled. I had feared and dreaded this from the start.' (226)

When Theo visited him he not only insisted on Vincent doing some painting but gave him some extra money to buy the right materials. Vincent wanted some reassurance from Theo that he could paint, that he could do it, 'I should only want the assurance that they are worth the brushes, the paint and the canvas, and that it is not throwing money away to do them, but that they are worth what they cost. In that case I should even work on them with great ambition.' (227) Once he dared to try, thanks to Theo's pressure, and found himself capable, he was tremendously relieved, 'To tell you the truth, it surprised me a little. I had expected the first things to be a failure . . . but . . . they are not bad at all, and I repeat, it surprises me a little.' (225) He attributed his success, probably rightly, to having concentrated so much on drawing and perspective earlier.

Once again, as we see, it was through Theo's agency that Vincent took fully the all-important step from drawing to painting and colour, a fact that he acknowledged by saying, 'Your coming made it possible for me', otherwise I would have kept exclusively to black and white and to the outline a little longer. But now I have launched my boat.' (223) And, 'During the few days since you left, I have made some experiments with painting . . . I must tell you that painting does not seem so strange to me as you would perhaps suppose.' (224)

He found colour 'a very strong means of expression . . . one can express tender things with it too, let a soft grey or green speak amid all the ruggedness' (224), and, 'There is something infinite in painting – I cannot explain it to you so well but it is so delightful just for expressing one's feelings. There are hidden harmonies or contrasts in colour which involuntarily combine to work together and which could not possibly be used in another way.' (226)

Vincent now complained again about the lack of understanding shown by the family in relation to him and especially to his work as a painter. Theo visited home at this time and reassured the parents about Vincent and especially about his work; this resulted in a nice letter from home that pleased Vincent a great deal. He wrote to his brother, 'I particularly thank you for the way you spoke, though it seems to me you said more good about me than I yet deserve.' (227) This led to some new timid attempts to win his father's admiration and approval. He sent him a lithograph of an old man but the father criticized it. Then he sent a new drawing of it taking into account his father's criticisms. He explained to

Theo that he did not do this because he thought the father was right in his criticisms but just to please him. 'Now I know how you like to have it, I will try and make it that way for you.' (263) He was disappointed because not even then did he feel he had succeeded, 'Father didn't exactly write that he didn't like it, but it was between the lines.' (263)

Now Theo became involved with a woman. She was unwell and he had to help her financially, so that it was not possible for him to send Vincent more money than usual as Vincent, latterly, had been asking him to do, and as he continued to ask, probably as an unconscious reaction to Theo's relationship with the woman. On a conscious level he answered 'Yes I am rather hard up and wish it were possible but do not deprive her for my sake.' (260) Nevertheless in the letters that followed he kept pressing frequently for more money. He was both cautious and ambivalent in his advice to Theo about this woman. To start with he did not think it a good idea for Theo to marry her and gave him back the advice Theo himself had given Vincent when he wanted to marry Christine: 'I remember a saying of yours last year which I thought very correct and true, "Marriage is such a queer thing." Yes, indeed, it certainly is. Then you said to me, "Do not marry her", and I admitted then that circumstances were such that it was better not to talk about it for the time being. And you know that since then I have not mentioned it again, but she and I have remained true to each other. And just because I cannot think you were wrong in saying then, "Do not marry her", I give you your own words to consider; and besides, you will think of it yourself, for it is not I who say so, but you yourself. And I remind you of it only because I think it was well it didn't take place at once. Don't let that idea go, for it is a good thing for love to ripen, so that marriage becomes subordinate to it. It is safer and it doesn't hurt anybody.' (261) Yet a few days later he would write, 'I wish from the bottom of my heart that she might become your wife, for a woman turns life into something so very different . . . And in my opinion an infinite and profound happiness – for you as well as for her – would be within reach because of the consciousness of not being alone any more. For it is sometimes bitterly hard for us men, too, that being alone.' (267)

Curiously enough at times during these last months in The Hague there was still occasionally some hesitation as to his becoming a painter. 'Painting is not my principal object, and perhaps I will be ready for illustrating sooner all by myself than if somebody, who wouldn't think of illustrations at all, advised me.' (292) Similarly he frequently expressed his need for reassurance from his brother and his wish to please him. 'One thing I hope more than anything else is that when you come, you will find that I have made progress and that there is some good in my work. From time to time you have written me that you found something in it; I don't think you were mistaken . . . Yes, that is the very first thing which I value: that you who from the very beginning have done so much – nay everything – for my work may continue to find some good in it. If I can bring this about, your visit would make me forget all the cares of the whole year.' (295)

His relationship to his father during this period remained severely strained and there are clear signs of his still extremely ambivalent feelings towards him. The negative ones certainly found full expression but there was, surprisingly enough, no lack of positive concern. His ambivalence shows particularly clearly when he pleads with Theo so that the latter will not hurt the father's feelings. Thus he says, referring to his father's objection to his and Theo's love affairs with prostitutes, 'Clergymen are the most ungodly people in society and dry materialists. Perhaps not right in the pulpit, but in private matters.' (288) But he also writes to Theo, 'Father is an old man and deserves to be cheered up if possible . . . you must act as you think right, but don't be angry with father if he is mistaken.' (291) He had many expenses in spite of his frugality, which made the money situation extremely difficult during all this period. Frequently food was short and he had to go without eating, feeling weak and faint, 'Again and again I have put off taking some nourishing food because I had to provide for others and for the work.' [painting materials] (304) Of course the economic limitations led to difficulties with Christine and this further pushed Vincent to ask Theo not only to keep up his economic help but to increase it too. Theo explained to him that his income had to be divided among no less than six persons. Vincent wrote, 'The division of your income, directly and indirectly, among no less than six persons is certainly remarkable. But the subdivision of my 150 francs among four human beings, with all the expenses for models, drawing and painting material, house rent, is also rather remarkable, isn't it? If those 150 francs could be increased by the work next year – I reckon the year begins with your visit – that would be delightful. We must find ways and means.' (304) Theo then suggested that Vincent could try to offer some of his work for sale to help matters out but at the same time criticized his untidy, discreditable appearance as something of an obstacle in this direction, remarking on how he and his father felt ashamed to take walks with him because of it.

Vincent found approaching people with his work a near impossibility. 'I am so afraid that the steps I might take to introduce myself would do more harm than good, and I wish I could avoid it . . . It is practically always so painful for me to speak to other people.' (312) And, 'The future would seem brighter if I were less awkward in my dealings with people. Without you, finding buyers for my work would be almost impossible; with you, it will eventually be possible.' (305) In the end he pleads with his brother to leave things as they are and not to force him to try and offer his work for sale: 'If possible, let me go on as I have up to now. If not, and if you want me to take my work around to different people, I shall not refuse to do so if you think it better.

'But, brother dear, human brains cannot bear everything; there is a limit . . . Trying to go and speak to people about my work makes me more nervous than is good for me. And what is the result ? Rejection, or being put off with fair promises. It would not make me nervous if it were you, for instance – you know me and I am used to speaking with you.' (315)

He is concerned that he is such a burden to his brother. 'If you stagger under it, tell me so plainly.' (312). He could go to London 'at once to work at *n'importe quoi*, even carrying parcels, and I will leave art till better times, at least the painting and having a studio.' (312) Theo in the end writes a reassuring letter to Vincent who answers 'I can hardly tell you how pleased I am with what you say about my work, I am glad you are of the opinion that it would be the wrong policy to undertake some outside job at the same time.' (316)

It is of interest to note that in Letter 309 Vincent talks of a premonition he frequently has that he will not live many more years: 'If I think of that in a coldly calculating manner, as if I were making an estimate of something, it is in the nature of things that I cannot possibly know anything definite about it.

'But in comparison with various persons whose lives one might happen to know, or in comparison with some people with whom one is supposed to have many things in common, one can draw some conclusions which are not completely without foundation. Therefore as to the time ahead in which I shall still be able to work, I think I may safely presume: that my body will keep a certain number of years *quand bien meme* – a certain number, between six and ten, for instance. I can assume this the more safely as at present there is no immediate *quand bien meme*.

'But for the present, such calculations are irrelevant; as I said, one can only take plans for a period of between five and ten years into account. I do not intend to spare myself, nor to avoid emotions or difficulties – I don't care much whether I live a longer or a shorter time; besides, I am not competent to take care of my physique the way a physician, for instance can.

'So I go on like an ignoramus who knows only this one thing: "In a few years I must finish a certain work.".' (309) His premonition will prove quite accurate. He has only about seven years more to live during which time he will certainly manage to make good his words in the above paragraph.

Vincent now started to acknowledge in his letters that the relationship with Christine was taking a turn for the worse. At first he blamed most of the difficulties he had with Christine on her mother and her family. They complained that he had too little money – which of course was true since he did not earn anything and was completely dependent on Theo's allowance of about 150 francs a month for all the expenses. Then they said that he did not really want her, that he was only using her for posing and that he would finally leave her in the cold. 'All these things were secretly discussed behind my back, and at last the woman told me.' (288) He reassured her that he would never leave her unless she turned to prostitution again, but Christine herself was growing increasingly dissatisfied; at times her violent mischievious bad temper was such that it was almost unbearable for him. 'I can tell you, I am sometimes in despair.' (288) Vincent was now not only having difficulties with Christine and her family but was under increasing pressure from Theo to leave the woman.

He had been with her over a year and had grown very fond of Christine's little boy who was now a year old. 'He is the merriest jolliest child you can imagine.' (297) He nevertheless still found joy and consolation in his difficulties, financial and otherwise, in the relationship to this woman and the children. 'When I am with them and the little boy comes creeping towards me on all fours, crowing for joy, I haven't the slightest doubt that everything is right. How often that child has comforted me.

'When I'm home, he can't leave me alone for a moment; when I'm at work, he pulls at my coat or climbs up against my leg till I take him on my lap. In the studio, he crows at everything, plays quietly with a bit of paper, a bit of string, or an old brush; the child is always happy. If he keeps this disposition all his life, he will be cleverer than I.' (306)

He pleaded with Theo to allow her to come to Drenthe with him, away from her family if she so wished, otherwise he would go alone. He wrote, 'But if she wants to come with me, do let her. Leaving her means driving her back to prostitution – how can this be done by the same hand that tried to save her?' (317) Shortly afterwards Vincent was finally under the impression that Christine was going to leave him and was going back to prostitution. He reacted to this by quickly deciding to leave her and he moved away on his own to Drenthe. He sent to his father the news about his leaving Christine at the same time. He arrived there in September 1883 and remained for about three months. 'You may depend on it that whatever may happen to her, I neither can nor ever will live with her again, for she is incapable of doing what she ought to do.' (319)

The separation from Christine was a severe blow to Vincent and in no way seems to have helped him. He felt quite miserable and alone; he was still very fond of her and the children. He wrote the following moving passage to Theo: 'Theo, when I meet on the heath such a poor woman with a child on her arms, or at her breast, my eyes get moist. It reminds me of her, her weakness; her untidiness, too, contributes to making the likeness stronger.

'I know that she is not good, that I have an absolute right to act as I do, that I could not stay with her back there, that I really could not take her with me, that what I did was even sensible and wise, whatever you like; but, for all that, it cuts me right through when I see such a poor little figure feverish and miserable and it makes my heart melt inside.' (324)

❧ 9 ❧

MOURNING CHRISTINE
The Drenthe Period: September – November 1883

VINCENT arrived in Drenthe heartbroken and discouraged. He feels uneasy and lonely, 'I cannot hide from you that I am overcome by a feeling of great anxiety, depression, a *je ne sais quoi* of discouragement and despair more than I can tell. And if I cannot find comfort, it will be too overwhelming' (328) . . . 'the fate of the woman and the fate of my poor little boy and the other child cut my heart to shreds.' (328)

He misses the children and Christine and though trying to keep control, he is full of regret at having left her. He would like to take refuge in his work but he does not have enough materials and their is no money. He wants an assurance that the money will come regularly. 'Before I begin – I do not distrust or suspect you, but it is a measure of commonsense – I repeat, before I begin (and I ask it because not very long ago you wrote me about being distressed yourself and being afraid of troubles and calamities in the future) can you assure me that the usual remittance will not be lacking?' (329) He continues, 'You must not be angry with me for writing the way I do. I came here in too much of a hurry, and only now I feel what I lack, and that I acted rather rashly – but what else could I do? I feel unexpressibly melancholy without my work to distract me, as you will understand, and I must work and work hard, I must forget myself in my work, otherwise it will crush me. I repeat, I do not distrust you in the slightest, but my experience forbids me to undertake an excursion without knowing what I can count on. So speak absolutely openly, for my decision depends on it, and, at all events, I will suit my actions to the circumstances.' (329) Though at this point he looks on his having left Christine as his own decision, in a few months he will be accusing Theo, perhaps not without reason, of having put pressure of an economic nature on him to force the break with her. Again, as we have mentioned, he is deeply moved at the sight of a mother and her child. He rages against clergymen – especially his father – and their lack of human warmth. He compares them unfavourably with pigs. Pigs at least make no disturbance; they are in their place and in harmony with their surroundings and 'before the clergymen of the type I saw here reach the cultural and rational level of ordinary pigs, they must improve considerably . . . Now any pig is better, as far as I can see'. (332)

Vincent, while at Drenthe, recommended an intense campaign to convince Theo that he too ought to become a painter and come and live with him. He had suggested this before but less vehemently. The campaign was triggered off by the fact that Theo had mentioned that he was having serious difficulties at work and that his dismissal was not impossible. His arguments are in no way reality-adapted and little rational consideration is given to the fact that Theo is the economic support not only of himself and of Vincent but of other members of the family as well. Vincent feels extremely lonely and now that he has given up Christine for his brother's sake he practically demands that Theo come and live with him, as if to take Christine's place. He writes, 'But I cannot help imagining the future, when I should no longer be alone, but you and I, painters, working together as comrades here in this moorland'. (332) He feels that by taking such a step Theo will not create 'any more disturbance than a piece of peat rolling from one place to another'. (332) He insists 'I believe that being alone in a region [Drenthe] would handicap one and make one dull for want of company. And I personally long very much for your company' (337), and 'In my opinion, it would be an error of judgment if you continued doing business in Paris. So the conclusion is: both brothers painters.' (338) He points out examples among the old masters and the moderns of brother painters. He thinks that by working together one will encourage the other and many periods of melancholy may be avoided, 'for me alone it is almost too big. I almost lack the courage to go on alone. I need a person to talk things over with – who knows what a picture is'. (339)

The possibility of his going to Paris is mentioned, Vincent

welcomes it because he will be less alone but no further action is taken in this respect.

In the end Vincent is in despair about money because Theo has not sent it to him, and is feeling unwell and nervous. He is forced to ask his father for a loan and decides to go for a short time to his family now living at Nuenen. In fact he stayed there for two years and never came back to Drenthe.

❧ 10 ❧

HIS FATHER'S DEATH
The Nuenen Period: December 1883 – November 1885

HARDLY had he arrived home than he was unhappy because he thought the family had not changed their basic attitude towards him. They were kind and cordial but showed no remorse whatsoever at having banished him from home two years earlier. 'Their cordial reception grieves me – their indulgence without acknowledging their error is, for me, perhaps worse than the error itself.' (345) He is as usual particularly bitter towards his father in whose mind 'there was not then, there is not now, the faintest shadow of a doubt that what he did was the right thing.' (345) He 'does not know remorse like you and me and any man who is human.

'Father believes in his own righteousness, whereas you and I and other human creatures are imbued of the feeling that we *consist* of errors and efforts of the lost souls'. (345)

He feels he is considered and treated like a dog, 'they feel the same dread of taking me in the house as they would about taking a big rough dog. He would run into the room with wet paws – and he is so rough'. He continues, 'All right – but the beast has a human history, and though only a dog, he has a human soul, and even a very sensitive one, that makes him feel what people think of him, which an ordinary dog cannot do.' (346) And, 'The dog feels that if they keep him, it will only mean putting up with him and tolerating him "*in this house*", so he will try to find another kennel. The dog is in fact Father's son, and has been left rather too much in the streets, where he could not but become rougher and rougher . . . And then – the dog might bite – he might become rabid, and the constable would have to come to shoot him . . . The dog is not only sorry that he did not stay away, for it was less lonely on the heath than in this house, not withstanding all the kindness. The dog's visit was a weakness . . . (that) he will avoid committing in the future.' (346) He will conclude, 'In short, this is what Father is – he is "a stupid one".' (348)

He refuses to contribute any money at home from the monthly allowance he receives from Theo. He needs the money to pay for his painting materials. He wants nothing to do with an economic arrangement with his father, if Theo wants to do it 'let it be purely a matter between you and Father, in which I am not involved'. (315a)

During this period his mother writes of him: 'How is it possible to behave so unkindly ? If he has wishes for the future, let him exert himself, he is still young enough; it is almost impossible to bear it. I think he wants a change – perhaps he might find something that would give him inspiration. Here it is always the same, and he never speaks to anyone.' (XXXVIII)

He is annoyed with his brother and thinks that perhaps it is better if he and Theo separate 'for a time, as friends . . . staying together would end badly if things went on like this'. (355a) As we can see the relations between the two brothers are going through difficult times and will still worsen for a time. Vincent is resentful for many reasons, especially for having had to give up Christine – he will come quite openly to blame this on the lack of his brother's support and even more on his direct pressure to abandon her. There was also the fact that Theo did not decide to come to Drenthe and live with Vincent in order to become a painter as the latter had demanded. Furthermore Theo had defended the father and at times taken his side against Vincent's attacks.

In any case he had been longing to see Christine and finally did so 'finding her in such a condition that my heart melted in my breast – that – it will remain something insuperable between you and me – *unless she can still be saved*'. (305a) He accuses Theo of having been frivolous, of having spoken on insufficient grounds when going against Christine adding that Theo had, in common with their father, been cruel in his wordly wisdom. He is aware of the risks he takes arguing with Theo on whom he is totally dependent for money and warns him against his 'politics'. If Theo had behaved differently in the Christine affair 'things would not have come to such a pass that I had to give up' (350a); a few days later he adds, 'In the long run I should prefer to do without your support, however much your help means to me, to keeping it on condition that I act contrary to what I think right'. (351)

Vincent's resentment rises again at the possibility, mentioned earlier, of a lawsuit to deprive him of his legal rights; he tries to provoke his father by threatening to go back to Christine and even marry her, while at the same time he reassures Theo that he would not do so. He writes to his brother that occasionally he thinks of marriage as very desirable but 'certainly not as regards the woman I lived with'. (351)

He wants to sell his work in order to earn more money. He would like to earn enough to pay his working expenses and in this way Theo could give his mother the money he is now getting.

The mother has just had an accident and fractured her leg. At this time Vincent is a great help to the family and looks after his mother a great deal. He even gives his father some of the money he would normally have spent on painting materials. Relationships at home improve altogether for the time being.

He begins to accuse his brother of not really trying to sell his work at all. 'I must make my own way, Theo, and with you I am exactly as far as I was a few years ago; what you say about my work now, "It is almost saleable, but" – is literally the same as what you wrote me when I sent you my Brabant sketches from Etten.' (358) He now even doubts his brother's sincerity in praising his work and complains of receiving only economic help; if Theo thinks him not advanced enough he should do 'something to help (him) to make progress . . . bring me into contact with some other painter . . . some sign that proved to me that you really believed in my progress, or wanted to further it.' (358) And, 'Brotherly, or not brotherly, if you can give me nothing more than financial help, you may keep that too'. (358) He revolts violently against his economic dependence and passivity, because he feels it lays him open to pressure and manipulations, as in the case of Christine, 'it has become evident to me that – although you say you leave me absolutely free – as a matter of fact, when for instance I have some affair with a woman which you and others do not approve of, perhaps rightly so, a thing that once in a while I do not give a damn about, there comes such a little tug at the financial bridle in order to make me feel that it is "in my own interest" to conform to your opinion.

93

'In the matter of that woman you also got what you wanted, but . . . but I am damned if I care to receive a little bit of money if I have to practice morality in exchange.' (358) He makes similar statements in several letters at this point and insists that his ability to get along financially must be dependent only on his work and not on his private life. He refuses to become Theo's protégé and will accept his brother's help in the future only on the basis that it is considered as a money payment for his work which thus becomes Theo's property.

All this time Vincent had gone on working intensively and had continued his painted studies in oil. Theo on his part had been trying to interest Vincent in impressionism and its clearer palette. Vincent responded, 'As to my own palette, you will not find silvery tones in my work done here, but rather brown ones (bitumen, for instance, and bister), which I do not doubt some people will disapprove of' (368), and somewhat later, 'from what you told me about "impressionism", I have indeed concluded that it is different from what I thought, but it's not quite clear to me what it really is'. (371)

Sometime around August 1884 Margot Begemann with whom he had become friendly attempted to commit suicide by taking poison 'after she had had a discussion with her family and they slandered her and me, and she became so upset that she did it (in a moment of decided mania, I think)'. (375) The Begemann family was opposed to the relationship and suspected *'she had done something frightful. And this without having done anything she ought not to have done'*. (377)

Vincent got a terrific fright since it happened while they were away alone in the fields. She fell to the ground with spasms, jerks and convulsions, mumbling all kinds of things. In the end Vincent had to fetch her brother. He was prepared to marry her and left it to her doctor to decide, the latter advising that she was too weak to marry. This incident, that could not but create more ill feeling between Vincent and the family, did not result in any further developments. In later years Vincent would still remember Margot Begemann and send her one of his painted studies as a present through one of his sisters.

The question of money, of needing some extra money, of not being able to make ends meet, is a constantly recurring theme in Vincent's letters leading him at times to abuse his brother. 'I do not intend to exchange the *chance* (although it be no more than a chance) of pulling through on my own for the certainty of a protection that is a bit stifling after all.' (378) He rages too because his brother does not lift a finger 'to find an opening for me with one of the illustrated papers, so that I can earn something'. (378)

Vincent was not by any means extravagant in spending the money his brother sent. He was described by those who went on rambles with him as 'starving like a true Bohemian'. (435c) His diet was mostly dry bread and cheese . Meat was out of the question for weeks on end, Vincent saying jokingly, 'It won't go bad on the road'. He was accustomed to this and refused anything better saying, 'No, that would be coddling myself too much: bread and cheese is what I am used to'. (435c) He had started to drink and liked to carry some brandy in his flask. He did not spend money on clothes for himself either. In fact the money went mainly towards his painting expenses, 'not to make them [the expenses] is not always the best policy, for if one hesitates to take models or to buy the necessary painting materials, no serious work could result.

'And as things are getting worse and worse for me instead of better they have finally got so bad that I really must complain.' (421)

In view of all the previous complaints it is interesting to see Vincent's reaction when his brother asked him for some paintings that he considered suitable to send for an important exhibition at the Salon. He had been accusing Theo of not furthering his work, of not trying to show it, of making no attempts to sell it, but now that Theo offered to exhibit it he withdrew. This is a pattern of behaviour that would repeat itself frequently in times to come and that hints at a peculiar combination in Vincent of a fear of failure and a fear of success. He answers, 'I appreciate your being willing to do so . . . had I known it six weeks ago, I should have tried to send you something for the purpose.

'Now I have nothing that I should care to send in.' (395) For similar reasons his description of the following episode is of interest. He once gave away a painting when it was admired, though presumably he could have sold it. He had taken it to a friend's house to see its general effect on the wall of the drawing room. 'Now, though that man has money, though he took a fancy to it, I felt such a glow of courage when I saw that it was good . . . *that I could not sell it*. But as he had a fancy for it, I gave it to him.' (431) (Shortly afterwards when he moved to Antwerp he tried to exhibit and to sell being again active in this respect and finding some minor galleries where his work was exhibited on commission).

Vincent and his father continued to quarrel frequently and violently. Then on April 26, 1885 his father died suddenly at the very door of the house when returning from a walk. There are remarkably few references in his letters to this event, in fact they appear only in Letters 397 and 398 as *en passant* comments. He says to Theo that, like him, he could not work as usual for the first days. 'Indeed, those were days we shall not easily forget. And yet the total impression was not terrible only solemn.' (397) In Letter 398 he refers to a still life he has just painted in the foreground of which appear his father's tobacco pouch and his pipe. No other reaction is noticeable, a remarkable fact indeed if we take into account the circumstances of the father's death and the state of the relationship between them. Vincent had managed to hide from himself for the moment any feelings of guilt. Nevertheless the full impact of his father's death was to show itself more clearly a few years later.

Nevertheless it was at this point immediately after the father's death that Vincent started to work on one of his most famous paintings, and certainly the most important one he had done so far: the first version of 'The Potato Eaters'. It is not without significance that this first great achievement was accomplished after the father's death.

Vincent's relationship with Rappard, a fellow painter with whom he had corresponded in amicable terms for some time, came to an end because of Rappard's rather harsh criticism of a lithograph of 'The Potato Eaters'. He could not understand Rappard's behaviour and concluded that he must have been influenced against him by Tersteeg and Mauve by whom he still tended to feel persecuted in a paranoid way. 'Van Rappard, with whom I have been friends for years . . . wrote me a letter, so haughty and so full of insults and so clearly written after he had been in The Hague that I am almost sure I have forever lost him as a friend.' (413) Vincent's assumption was correct; the correspondence and friendship with Rappard was over. After Vincent's death Rappard was to regret the break, attributing it to a misunderstanding.

It should be noted that Vincent's extreme sensitivity to criticism applied only in the case of those he considered his equals or superiors. Otherwise he was quite capable of a great deal of tolerance. Thus, when Anton Kerssemakers, a local man at Nuenen and an amateur painter whose acquaintance Vincent had made, came to see his studio and criticized his drawing Vincent did not react in anger, 'he only laughed a little and said quietly, "later on you will think differently".' (435c)

For a short time Vincent associated at Etten with a number of people who were interested in painting as a hobby, especially a tanner, and a man by the name of Herman who had many beautiful 'old jars and other antiques' (387) that Vincent used occasionally for his still lives.

A painter friend of Theo, Serret, criticized Vincent's drawing on the basis that he did not always give enough attention to correct proportion and anatomical detail. Vincent argued that he wanted his figures to be *felt* like the figures of Israel, Daumnier or Lhermitte: in those figures the proportions are almost '*arbitrary*, the anatomy and structure often quite wrong "in the eyes of the academician". But it will *live*'. (418) He begs Theo, 'Tell Serret that I should be desperate if my figures were correct, tell him that I do not want them to be academically correct, tell him that I mean: if one photographs a digger, he certainly would not be digging then. Tell him that I adore the figures by Michelangelo though the legs are undoubtedly too long, the hips and the backsides too large. Tell him that, for me, Millet and Lhermitte are the real artists for the very reason that they do not paint things as they are, traced in a dry analytical way, but as they – Millet, Lhermitte, Michelangelo – feel them. Tell him that my great longing is to learn to make these very incorrrectnesses, those deviations, remodellings, changes in reality, so that they may become, yes, lies if you like – but truer than the literal truth.' (418)

After his father's death he runs into more difficulties at home with his mother and especially with his sister Anna, he plans to move out of the house into the adjacent studio. Relationships continue to be more or less difficult and in the end his unconscious death wishes against his mother reach consciousness in the guise of a presentiment. Then he writes to Theo, 'Would it greatly amaze you – let's suppose those at home intend to move between March and May next – would it greatly amaze you if something happened to Mother before that time? Now and then this thought occurs to me when I go there' (432), and, 'For the rest, however, one might say that Mother is looking particularly well. But there is something that makes me think of what I told you. I don't think it would be a bad idea at all if Mother made a few trips shortly, to Anna, to Amsterdam, to Cor – especially as she seems to be resolved on it and longs to see them all once more. But it might well be that she herself has a presentiment that at the same time it will be a leave-taking.' (432) In the end these phantasies of Vincent led to his mother's consulting her doctor who reassured the family that there was nothing wrong with her: in fact Vincent's mother outlived him by seventeen years. Such manifestations of Vincent's negative feelings towards his mother as the above phantasies, can be seen only occasionally throughout his life.

❧ 11 ❧

EXPULSION FROM THE ACADEMY
The Antwerp Period: November 1885 – February 1886

VINCENT departed from Nuenen after quarrelling with the family. He told his mother that he had no intention of writing and he did not tell her his new address. The mother found it through Theo and wrote to Vincent asking him to write to her, but he had no intention of doing so, since he felt he had not received proper treatment while at home. He wrote to Theo, 'Tell mother so, if you like, for I do not want to say a harsh word to her, but I positively decline to write. And mother is old, so I do not want to tell sharply that I refuse to write. Such things have happened to other painters too, and it is one of those things it is better to leave alone.' (438)

He again complains that the money he receives from Theo is insufficient to cover his bills for colours and models, let alone food, and when forced to make a choice he will go hungry and spend the money on materials. Painting is literally his only source of release and happiness; for this reason it has taken such a hold on him that he does not mind having a hot meal only occasionally, sometimes only once in several days, living on bread for the rest of the time.

We have to take into account as well the fact that through painting he can have a human contact, a relationship to people, thanks to his models. He has a tremendous longing for human warmth and company, but is aware at the same time of his complete inability to relate to others. His efforts in this direction usually lead to disappointment, frustration and suffering. In his hunger for human contact, his models are his only link with the human race. Thus he says, 'As long as I am painting it is more

99

than enough, but a feeling of weakness comes when the models have left'. (442)

Frequently he goes to popular balls to see the heads of women, soldiers and sailors, and since he cannot take part with these people, he passes a whole evening in watching them enjoy themselves.

Theo, on the other hand is going through a difficult financial time and is forced to warn Vincent again that he cannot send the extras he is asking for, and may even be forced to reduce Vincent's monthly allowance to satisfy his own innumerable creditors. Vincent retorts, 'I know, Theo, that you may also be rather hard up. But your life has never been so hard as mine has these last ten or twelve years. Can't you make allowance for me when I say, Perhaps it has been long enough ?' (444) He argues that surely his needs are more important than those of Theo's creditors, 'I beg you most kindly but urgently – let one of your creditors wait, i.e. at least for 50 francs (they can stand it, do not be afraid), but please do not let it be me, for even then it will still be tough for me'. (442)

In a further attempt to come into contact with people, he applies to join the Academy painting class: 'People are more important than anything else' (444), 'At all events, it is an attempt to come into contact with people'. (445) His short stay at the Academy has been described by several witnesses. Richard Baseleer told Tralbaut[1] that the news of Vincent's arrival spread like a wild fire, 'Some sort of savage had dropped in'. (458a) Victor Hageman, himself a pupil in the drawing class, stated: 'I remember quite well that weather-beaten nervous restless man who crashed like a bombshell into the Antwerp academy, upsetting the director, the drawing master and the pupils'. (458a) He painted 'feverishly, furiously, with a rapidity that stupefied his fellow students . . . his colours literally dripped from his canvas on to the floor'. (458a) When the teacher saw his work he demoted Vincent to the drawing class. Shortly afterwards in one of the drawing classes the students were presented with a cast of the Venus de Milo to copy. Vincent strongly accentuated the breadth of the hips. Again, when the teacher 'saw this, he tore Van Gogh's drawing sheet with the furious corrective strokes of his crayon, reminding his disciple of the inviolable canons of his

[1] Tralbaut, Mark Edo., *Van Gogh a Pictorial Biography*, Thames and Hudson, London.

art'. (438a) Vincent flew into a rage, 'So you don't know what a young woman is like, God damn you! A woman must have hips and buttocks and a pelvis in which she can hold a child!' (458a) Hageman commented that this was the last lesson Vincent took – or gave – at the Academy. Another account has it that he was further demoted to drawing 'noses and ears'. Be that as it may, this brought about the end of his days in the academy at Antwerp.

He wants now to go to Paris; Theo agrees, not without some trepidation since he fears that Vincent will soon be disappointed in him. Theo plans to move to a larger flat some time in June or July but Vincent wants to go as soon as possible. When Theo suggests that he go to Nuenen to his family for a short period before coming to Paris, Vincent dislikes this plan.

Vincent on his side is distressed unconsciously too. He needs some protection against his unconscious homosexual phantasies now that he is going to live with his brother and such unconscious conflicts find expression in the following letter where he proposes that they should both marry as soon as possible. 'Now that we are discussing things, I want to tell you to begin with that I wish both of us might find a wife in some way or other before long, for it is high time, and if we should wait too long, we should not be the better for it.

'But I say this in all calmness. However, it is one of the first requisites for our more hygienic life. And I mention it because in that respect we may have to overcome an enormous difficulty, on which a great deal depends. And herewith I break the ice on the subject; we shall always have to return to it. And in the intercourse with women one especially learns so much about art.' (453)

In the end Vincent departs suddenly for Paris without informing Theo beforehand. He stays in Theo's small flat at the Rue de Laval until June, when they move to a larger flat at the 54 Rue Lepic in Montmartre.

❧ 12 ❧

VINCENT AND THEO TOGETHER
IN PARIS
The Second Paris Period: March 1886 – February 20, 1888

THIS 'Paris' period is of the greatest significance with regard to Vincent's further development as a painter and to the influence that impressionism and the close contact with many of its most important exponents had on him. Unfortunately relatively little is known about this period: the brothers were now living together so that our main source of information, their correspondence, is non-existent but for the occasional letter written when Theo was away travelling.

A few significant facts are nevertheless known. Vincent went to Cormon's Studio for three or four months but was soon dissatisfied and left.

From the beginning of his stay in Paris he seemed to improve a great deal. Theo wrote a reassuring letter to his mother explaining how much Vincent had changed for the better. He was making progress in his work and had some friends! Theo concluded, 'I think the most difficult period is past, and he will find his way'. Such hopes were soon shattered.

At the time Theo was involved in a relationship with an apparently rather disturbed girl referred to as 'S'. It was not a satisfactory relationship, and Vincent felt that, though his brother must part company with the girl, he ought not to be harsh about it in case it drove her to suicide or madness. He came out with the peculiar proposal that if Theo and S. agreed he would be prepared to make an 'amicable arrangement' consisting in his taking S. off Theo's hands and if necessary even agreeing to a *marriage de raison* with her. This apparently incongruous proposal will be discussed later on in relation to Vincent's own nervous breakdown and final suicide in which contexts it can be better understood.[1] Vincent commented in a letter to his brother while the latter was visiting home that it would please their mother if Theo married. As for himself, it seems that now he was finding some incompatibility between married life, family life, even sexual interests and his work as a painter. He was beginning to decide for the latter. 'I already feel old and broken, and yet still enough of a lover not to be a real enthusiast for painting' (462), and 'as for me – I feel I am losing the desire for marriage and children, and now and then it saddens me that I should be feeling like that at thirty-five, just when it should be the opposite. And sometimes I have a grudge against this rotten painting. It was Richepin who said somewhere: "The love of art makes one lose real love".' (462)

During his stay in Paris Vincent took to drinking heavily and was rather difficult and quarrelsome. He was on more than one occasion involved in fights and in his letters he refers specifically to one that took place at the Cafe Tambourin whose lady owner seems to have been his mistress for some time. He shows no sense whatsoever of limits and very little reality adaptation. Andres Bonger, whose sister was to marry Theo some years later, himself a close friend of Theo who frequently stayed at the Van Gogh's flat or had meals there, once commented, when Theo was ill, 'Theo is still looking frightfully ill; he literally has no face left at all. The poor fellow has many cares. Moreover, his brother is making life rather a burden to him, and reproaches him with all kinds of things of which he is quite innocent . . .

'I think I told you last summer what a queer life this brother has led. The man hasn't the slightest notion of social conditions. He is always quarrelling with everybody. Consequently Theo has a lot of trouble getting along with him.' (462a) Theo himself was to write to his younger sister: 'My home life is almost unbearable. No one wants to come and see me any more because it always ends in quarrels, and besides, he is so untidy that the room looks far from attractive. I wish he would go and live by himself. He sometimes mentions it, but if I were to tell him to go away, it would just give him a reason to stay; and it seems I do him no good. I ask only one thing of him, to do me no harm; yet by his staying he does so, for I can hardly bear it.' He continued: 'It

[1] p. 180.

seems as if he were two persons: one, marvellously gifted, tender and refined, the other, egoistic and hard-hearted. They present themselves in turns, so that one hears him talk first in one way, then in the other, and always with arguments on both sides. It is a pity that he is his own enemy, for he makes life hard not only for others but also for himself.' (XLI)

When the sister advised Theo to leave Vincent to his own devices, Theo could not bring himself to do it. He thought that Vincent would do well in the end as an artist and that it was a pity to hinder him by withdrawing his support.

It was at this time and during one of his visits to Amsterdam that Theo was to make the acquaintance of Jo (A. Bonger's sister) who was to become his wife.

Vincent met many painters with some of whom he exchanged 'studies'. He met Pisarro, Tolouse-Lautrec, Bernard, Laval, Hartrick, Levens, Gauguin and many others. Of them all, Gauguin was destined to play a major role in Vincent's life and art.

Early in 1888 Vincent was ill for a short time; after recovering he decided to go to Arles where he arrived towards the end of February.

ᔥ 13 ᔥ

THE YELLOW HOUSE
The Arles Period: St Remy and Auvers-sur-Oise
February 21, 1888 – May 8, 1889

IN February 1888 Vincent goes to the south of France, to Arles, where he is to stay for approximately a year and three months. This Arles period is of the utmost significance in the life of the painter from both the psychological and the artistic points of view. His art finds now its fullest form of expression; he has achieved absolute mastery and paints much of his finest work. His psychological life and conflicts reach a similar climax which unfortunately marks the beginning of an extremely unhappy and disturbed period in his life running almost uninterruptedly to the end just a year and two months later in July 1890.

Vincent has now many cares and worries. Theo's health is not good and this is a source of concern for him. He complains occasionally about his own physical health; his digestion gives him some trouble and there is generally a slight hypochondriacal undercurrent. At times he complains of nervousness and anxiety. At times he feels excited, at others depressed. His isolation and loneliness at Arles are no great help either. 'Some days I still suffer from unaccountable, involuntary fits of excitement or else utter sluggishness, but that will pass as I get calmer.' (489) Sometimes after painting in a frenzy he finds his head so tired that 'the only thing to bring ease and distraction, in my case and other people's too, is to stun oneself with a lot of drinking or heavy smoking'. (507) He explains to Theo that instead of thinking of disastrous possibilities he throws himself completely into his work and 'if the storm within gets too loud, I take a glass too much to stun myself'. (513) In this way he is trying to fight his nervousness, his anxiety, his conflicts, his loneliness and misery. None of this is in itself much different from his previous general condition. The more severe disturbances are still to come.

What becomes almost unbearable at Arles is the feeling of loneliness. He deals with it as well as he can, he throws himself into his work. 'If I am alone – I can't help it but honestly I have less need of company than of furiously hard work, and that is why I am boldly ordering canvas and paints. It's the only time I feel I am alive, when I am drudging away at my work.

'If I had company, I should feel it less of a necessity; or rather I'd work at more complicated things.

'But alone, I only count on the exaltation that comes to me at certain moments and then I let myself run to extravagances.' (504) Similarly 'For loneliness . . . the unsatisfied need for kindness and sympathy – that is hard to bear . . . undermines us more than dissipation'. (489) He drinks a great deal, at times with the quite conscious purpose of being dulled by it as we have seen. He devises a scheme by means of which he and other painters would be able to stop living in rooms, in cafes, and the like. He conceives of a 'community of painters' all living under the same roof and pooling their resources. For this purpose he in the end rents a house at Arles – a house well known to all art lovers through several paintings, the yellow house, the house of friends. This house, he thinks, can mark the beginning of the community of painters. He hopes that at least Gauguin, who is going through rather difficult times economically, will come to live with him, since with the money he actually expends, or little more, two painters could live sharing a roof and other things. When Gauguin delays coming down to Arles from Pont Aven near Paris, Vincent, as on many other occasions, deals with his disappointment by means of denial. 'For the time being solitude does not worry me, and later on we shall find someone to keep me company and perhaps more than we want.' (541) And 'I think I shall end up not feeling lonesome in the house, and that during the bad days in the winter, for instance, and the long evenings, I shall find some occupation that will take all my attention. Weavers and basket-makers often spend whole seasons alone or almost alone, with their handicraft their only distraction.

'But what makes these people stay in one place is feeling at home, the reassuring familiar look of things. I'd certainly like company, but if I haven't got it, I shall not be unhappy because of it; then too the time will come when I shall have someone with me. I have little doubt of it. I think that if you were willing to put people up in your house too, you would find plenty of artists for whom the question of lodgings is a very serious problem.' (542)

Perhaps we can now understand better why he felt so strongly the need to draw human figures, why he used his monthly allowance to pay for models, even at the expense of going hungry for days on end. He said of the human figure, 'Altogether it is the only thing in painting that excites me to the depth of my soul, and which makes me feel the infinite more than anything else'. (516)

For the sake of clarity the rest of the Arles period, the St Remy period and the Auvers sur Oise period are now condensed in the chapters on 'Vincent's Mental Illness', 'The Two Empty Chairs', and 'Vincent's Suicide' that follow. There follow as well several auxiliary chapters to round up the arguments I have put forward at different points in the description.

⚡ 14 ⚡

THE REACTION TO
THEO'S ENGAGEMENT

THE role of Theo's engagement and later marriage is of the utmost importance in Vincent's psychopathology. It justifies at this moment a chronological account of events and of Vincent's reaction to them in so far as this is possible. Nevertheless I will approach the question here in a rather descriptive and superficial manner only, so as to facilitate the understanding of its full significance for Vincent's unconscious and for the shaping of events to come in the chapter devoted to his illness.

Theo was engaged to and finally married Johanna Bonger a sister of Andres Bonger. The latter was known to Vincent from the Paris period when the three had lived together at Theo's flat. The engagement took place towards the end of 1888 and the wedding in April 1889. Much of Theo's correspondence has unfortunately not been preserved and this makes the reconstruction of events incomplete. Thus the reconstruction of when and how Vincent received the news has to be made on the basis of the comments that appear in his own letters to his brother on this subject. Furthermore we must take into account that Theo had been to Arles to see his brother because of the latter's mental breakdown in the last week of December 1888. It is of course conceivable that Theo kept silent about his engagement to Jo then because of Vincent's condition, but it is not possible to account for his apparent silence about his relationship to Jo earlier on. The first of Vincent's letters with comments about this was written on January 1, 1889 when he was recovering at the mental hospital in Arles from his first psychotic breakdown. It seems from that letter that Vincent was not clear about the situation though he may well have assumed it. He said there, 'I cannot tell you how glad I am that you have made peace, and even more than that, with the Bongers'. (566) In a letter written the following day, he writes again, 'I have read and re-read your letter about your meeting the Bongers. It is splendid'. (567) The following letter (568) is not dated but was written between the third and the sixth of January. He wrote it in the morning and in the evening wrote again (Letter 569). In the morning letter he says, 'I am very anxious to know how the Bongers are and if the relations with them continue. I hope so'. (568) In the evening letter one finds, 'On your part follow this meeting with the Bongers up quietly. I hope it will continue as a lasting friendship, and that perhaps it will be even more.' (569)

None of these comments are sufficiently clear as to the information he had received but it seems that official news of the engagement was on the whole unknown to him; this is a surprising fact since Theo was at that time already engaged to Jo who had been staying in Paris with her brother Andres for a while. On the other hand it seems to me evident from Vincent's letters and reactions that he sensed that something unusual was going on in his brother's life.

It was only on January 9th, that Vincent wrote acknowledging the arrival that very morning of a letter from Jo with the news. A letter from Theo with the same news arrived the same day, Vincent wrote, 'Even before receiving (this very moment) your kind letter, I had had a letter this morning from your fiancée announcing the engagement'. (596) In his next letter to Theo, a particularly long one written on January 17th, he does not refer to the engagement at all, a point to be noted and to be contrasted with his frequent references to the Bongers we have noted. Still, in the following letter no mention of the engagement is made, but for the acknowledgement of a note from Jo in the following dry sentence, 'Jo sent me a note in reply to my congratulations, it is very kind of her'. (572)

We can see in the letters how he slowly gets reconciled to the idea of Theo's engagement. This was very much facilitated by Jo's determined efforts to gain Vincent's sympathy and affection though obvious signs of his ambivalence were always to remain. He thinks that Theo owes it to his social position to get married; this has been after all his mother's wish for years – but he adds, 'so from me, your brother, you will not want banal congratulations and assurances that you are to be transported straight into paradise'. (573)

One of his immediate reactions, as used to happen whenever he felt anything threatening to the relationship with his brother, was to increase his demands for money. He wrote, 'Don't be too amazed if during the next month I shall be obliged to ask you for the month's money in full and some extra money as well'. (574) A little later in the same letter his unconscious motivation for the demand becomes clear. He must be reassured, at least for once, that Theo's marriage and Jo herself are not more important to his brother than he is. He said, 'The main thing is that I am asking categorically for two month's work [his monthly allowance from Theo] before making the arrangements which will have to be made at the time of your marriage'. (574) For the time after the marriage he asks only for the position of a painting employee of Theo and Jo, 'at least as long as there is enough to pay one'. (574) He finally asks in fact 500 francs, a rather large amount, especially in the circumstances. At the same time he makes the following remark, of special interest in view of his later suicide: 'You will have gone on being poor all the time in order to support me, but I will give you back the money or give up the ghost'. (574) Towards the end of his life as we will see, he did come to the conclusion that he was a burden to his brother and his family.

Between this point and the wedding he was to suffer two more psychotic breakdowns of which the second especially was triggered off by such events. Even around the time of the wedding Vincent was apparently not informed where the wedding was to take place. He was not certain if it was to be in Breda or Amsterdam. His ambivalence was again clearly noticeable in the following letter of congratulations he sent at the beginning of April: 'A few lines to wish you and your fiancée very good luck these days. It is a sort of nervous affliction of mine that on festive occasions I generally have difficulty in formulating good wishes, but you must not conclude from this that I wish you happiness less earnestly than anyone else as you know'. (583)

Naturally, during the honeymoon Theo did not write as frequently as usual and Vincent though able to understand this was affected by it. He wrote to his sister that he was longing for news from Theo, 'who seems to have been rather absorbed in his honeymoon, which is a good thing . . . but a month has gone by since I received a letter from him'. (W.12)

Towards the end of April he assumed (though he obviously had not heard from Theo and Jo for some time) that they might be back in Paris, and wished them much happiness. For a number of different reasons he decided now to go to live in an asylum. He was depressed, he felt lonely, and he wanted to save Theo further expenditure. He thought that 75 francs or so would suffice if he were interned; having to pay more would make him unhappy, since he feared that Theo and Jo could be short of money for their housekeeping needs. Theo was not far wrong when he wrote him about this plan, 'this idea is born of an exaggerated dread of causing me expenses and worry, and you consequently bother your head unnecessarily'. (T.6) Theo was shattered by this idea of his brother's and it is quite possible that this was to some degree Vincent's unconscious intention, though it was by no means the main determinant of his decision. Vincent further explained that he might not be writing as often as he used, advising his brother to transfer his affection for him to his wife as much as possible, thus if they corresponded less she would be a comfort to him. He reassured his brother, 'I assure you that I am much calmer now that I can tell myself that you have a companion for good. Above all, do not imagine that I am unhappy'. (586)

Once Theo and Jo were settled in Paris Vincent attributed to his mother a thought that must have been lurking in his own mind, 'Naturally very soon, or even now already, her mind [mother's] will be running on seeing you with a child. That is dead certain'. (587) We will have the opportunity later to see how Jo's pregnancy was to affect the course of events.

❧ 15 ❧

VINCENT'S MENTAL ILLNESS
Arles-St Remy-Auvers: December 1888 – July 1890

LIST OF SIGNIFICANT EVENTS
CONCERNING HIS ILLNESS

The First Crisis: Evening of December 24, 1889	Attempted attack on Gauguin – Cuts his ear lobe – Taken to Mental Hospital.
January 7, 1889	Out of Hospital; allowed to return to the 'yellow house'.
January 22, 1889	His friend Roulin the postman leaves Arles for Marseilles.
The Second Crisis: First Week of February 1889	Back to Hospital, delusions of being poisoned.
Some days later	Allowed back to 'yellow house' provisionally but still eating and sleeping at the Hospital.
The Third Crisis: February 24, 1889	Back to Hospital through petition of Arles' citizens.
Very end of March, beginning of April 1889	Theo's marriage.
After Theo's Wedding	Decides he wants to live in the sanatorium at St Remy.

Up to this point he has suffered three fainting fits but they cannot be dated.

May 1889 – May 1890	Voluntarily goes to the St Remy sanatorium.
July 5, 1889	Receives news of Jo's pregnancy. Jo expresses concern for Theo's health.
The Fourth Crisis: End of July and August 1889	New crisis (around the time of his exhibiting at The Independents).
September 1889	Dr Peyron writes to Theo stating Vincent has recovered.
The Fifth Crisis: End of November-December 1889	Another crisis a few days after returning to Arles. Disorder lasts a week.

O. THE REAPER

ainted towards the very end when he contemplated death, at least uncon-
:iously, as a liberation from all of his human misery. This reaper was for him
symbol of death. He wrote to his brother about the painting, 'I see in this
:aper—a vague figure fighting like a devil in the midst of the heat to get to the
nd of his task—I see in him the image of death . . . But there is nothing sad
bout his death, it goes its way in broad daylight with a sun flooding everything
ith a light of pure gold'. (Letter 604.) (See Chapter 20, Vincent's Suicide,
age 174.)

hoto by courtesy of the Amsterdam Municipal Museum

II. THE OLD MAN IN SORROW

This striking drawing vividly depicts an infinite depth of sadness, depression, sorrow and black despair. It is probably a symbolic allusion to himself.

Photo by courtesy of the Amsterdam Municipal Museum

The Sixth Crisis: February 24, 1890	Dr Peyron writes that Vincent is ill again. He had visited Arles again and was brought back from there ill. Crisis lasted until around April.
Second fortnight in May 1890	Arrives in Paris. Few days later moves to Auvers-sur-Oise.

IN discussing his mental illness we are confining ourselves to the Arles period. Earlier we have discussed at least the most important aspects of his emotional disturbances up to the present period. These of course constitute the background to the present developments.

Unfortunately there are no case histories or records available from the different doctors that were in charge of Vincent's care and treatment or from the mental institutions where he was secluded. Nevertheless there are a number of publications concerning the nature of Vincent's illness (see for example Dr G. Kraus, *Vincent Van Gogh and die Psychiatrie* and its possible diagnostic classification. There are wide variations and differences of opinion in this respect in the views expressed by different authors. They range from schizophrenia, through alcoholism to epilepsia. I hold the view, for a number of reasons, that the question of labelling his illness diagnostically is in itself irrelevant.

We are all familiar with the fact that diagnostic classifications in psychiatry are to say the least insufficient; at times in fact completely irrelevant and useless. They tend to be based on clinical descriptions and grouping and the link with the causative, etiological factors is rather loose and insufficient in many instances. The concepts of health and illness are obscure and difficult to define in the field of mental health; the limits between health and illness are frequently imprecise. According to a well-known view of Freud we step frequently from health into illness and back to health in an imperceptible manner.

I further hold the view that in this respect we are observing in Vincent's illness a process of emotional disturbance, of mental instability, which follows a long line of development in historical terms all through the painter's life. This view is supported by the impression, which I hope to substantiate, that many of his 'crises' during this period were determined by specific psychological stresses related to factors and events of an internal and external

H   113

nature. They play a relevant role in the triggering off of the various psychotic breakdowns at this particular moment in his life span.

There is the further problem, in that the assessment of psychopathology in the genius poses special questions. As Eissler remarks in his book on *Leonardo da Vinci*, 'It is no longer disputed that in the study of genius a surprisingly large amount of psychopathology is encountered. The question, however, has not been answered what connection exists between the genius' psychopathology and his achievements . . . Psychopathology, in general, is looked upon as defect, though most forms of psychopathology have a useful function in so far as they spare the psychic apparatus a damage that would be greater than that caused by the psychopathology (primary gain). Observation of the genius, however, suggests the possibility that psychopathology is indispensable to the highest achievements of certain kinds'. (Page 283).

We have discussed how the first known signs of serious distress which started with his trip to London, were presumably triggered off by his anxiety about the separation from his family and his country. They were seriously aggravated by the love disappointment of the Ursula affair during the first London period.

We saw then how the serious breakdown of Vincent's emotional stability and mental equilibrium led among other things to a severe regression and a breakdown in his ability to relate to others, in his reality adaptation and in his affective life. His behaviour was consequently affected and from having been a first-class employee and a most promising art dealer at the firm of Goupil he had to be dismissed because of his extreme, abnormal behaviour. Much of his behaviour and of his activities generally from then onwards must be understood partly as the expression of his ongoing emotional disturbance and partly as attempts at regaining his lost emotional stability and mental dynamic equilibrium, as attempts to reorganize his personality structure and his inner conflicts in new ways, finding new outlets for the forces in conflict, new sublimations, new forms of adaptation. At times he regained, if only partially, a better equilibrium between the forces in turmoil in his personality. At times these factors and conflicts broke through again, the new adaptive achievements crumbling down – sometimes partially, sometimes totally – and new efforts to regain some degree of inner stability were needed. It is in this light that different episodes in his life such as his turning towards religion, his efforts to become a parson, his missionary work with the miners at the Borinage, his becoming a painter, must be approached and understood. The final mental breakdown at Arles is thus the culmination of a long line of development that points distinctly to a more serious failure in his ability to cope with internal forces and with life in general.

We have to remain aware that the reconstructions of events here attempted must of necessity be incomplete. It is only possible to point to those factors that are clearly discernible in the information available; much remains unknown to us, much no doubt we have not been able to evaluate and understand sufficiently. Adding to the difficulties of reconstruction is the type of material available for study. Material obtained for example, in the analysis of patients is usually more conclusive, definite and illuminating than any letters could possibly be. Nevertheless, partly compensating for this shortcoming is the fact that in this type of study we have at our disposal the whole span of life of the person as it evolved, from its beginning to its end and this allows for a retrospective longitudinal study. To my mind this in itself well justifies this attempt. Further, the study of some of his paintings is illuminating as I hope to show later.

It is also to be regretted that Vincent was rather reluctant to write in any detail about his illness. He made occasional references to it of a rather vague and general nature and specifically begged his brother on more than one occasion not to ask for more details about his illness: he really preferred not to speak or even to think of it.

It will be remembered that it was in December 1888 that Theo got engaged to be married. It looks as if Theo had some apprehension as to Vincent's reactions to his engagement since in the sequence of the letters one detects the fact that for a short while Theo maintained some secrecy about his engagement and plans about marriage. One similarly detects that Vincent, who was extremely sensitive perceived that something was going on. He reacted to this with an intensification of his campaign to have Gauguin come to live with him at Arles. He may have been hoping unconsciously that the relationship to the powerful father figure of Gauguin would fill the vacuum that he began to feel in the relationship to his brother. Gauguin was to be a partial substitute for his brother and we will see in this chapter the later impact of Theo's marriage on the artist's life and psychological equilibrium. His reaction was indeed of catastrophic proportions. Consciously of course he was to rejoice at the news though he expressed as well some reservations, feeling rejected, threatened and abandoned by his brother. Many earlier conflicts were soon reactivated and his restlessness greatly increased. His unconscious hostility against Theo rose to a peak and finally broke through in an attack on Gauguin, triggered off by the thought that Gauguin too was planning to leave and abandon him just as Theo was doing.

Before this incident Vincent and Gauguin had been living together in the 'yellow-house' for only two months but the relationship was far from peaceful. They argued bitterly. Both men had quite personal, original and strong views about art that were bound to clash. Vincent had expressed the fear of being over-influenced by Gauguin, he feared literally being swallowed by him, and before his arrival worked solidly trying to secure a personality of his own in his paintings, a personality that would stand up to Gauguin's influence. Gauguin was an individualist – outspoken, critical and self-possesed with the ambitions of a leader. Further he liked to have followers. On October 20th he came to Arles from Port Aven where he was accustomed to have around him a number of artists who looked up to him, to the master. Vincent deeply admired Gauguin as an artist and was fascinated by his personality but he could not be a follower. This had always been a threat to him because of his unconscious passive tendencies and his wish to surrender, both complexes being especially strong and conflictive in relation to Gauguin. Furthermore he too was an individualist, outspoken, critical but far from self-possesed. On the contrary he was insecure and very sensitive to criticisms about his person and his paintings. Soon the two men clashed.

Vincent started to suspect Gauguin of wanting to leave and was distressed. He had always reacted with extreme distress and hostility to feeling neglected, rejected, unwanted and abandoned. He became more and more heated and aggressive. On one occasion he threw a glass of absinthe into Gauguin's face. According to Gauguin, on the evening of December 24, 1889 he went out of the house and Vincent followed him in the dark, armed with a razor. Gauguin became aware of being followed, turned around and looked at Vincent. The latter stopped and finally went away back to the yellow house where he severed the lower part of his ear lobe with the razor. He proceeded to wrap it up and took it as a present to the girl at the brothel that he used to visit occasionally.

Naturally there was a big upheaval, and Rachel, the girl to whom he had taken his wrapped ear, fainted. Vincent was taken back to the yellow house by his friend, the postman Roulin. There he was found later by the police in a state of unconsciousness having apparently bled profusely. He was taken to the mental hospital where he was delirious and suffered from a high temperature. After only a few days, on New Year's Day, he was able to write reassuring his brother that his psychical health was good and continued to improve, and that serenity was returning to his brain day by day.

There can be little doubt that the events so far described played an essential role in this first serious mental breakdown at Arles. Its timing is not less meaningful; it happened when Theo's formal engagement was being arranged, and of course it was bound to interfere with the plans for the marriage. Furthermore, it could not fail to bring Theo down to Arles as indeed it did. Theo was of course greatly distressed by his brother's condition and felt uncertain as what to do next. He wrote to his fiancée, 'As you know, he has long since broken with what is called convention. His way of dressing and his manners show directly that he is an unusual personality and people who see him say, "He is mad." To me it does not matter, but for Mother that is impossible. Then there is something in his way of speaking that makes people either like or dislike him strongly. He always has people around him who sympathize with him, but also many enemies. It is impossible for him to associate with people in an indifferent way; it is either one thing or the other. It is difficult even for those who are his best friends to remain on good terms with him, as he spares nobody's feelings. If I had time, I would go to him and that would do him good. If I can find somebody among the painters who would like to do it, I will send him. But those with whom he would like to go are somewhat afraid of him, a circumstance which Gauguin's visit did nothing to change.' Theo continued:

'Then there is another thing which makes me afraid to have

him come, here in Paris he saw so many things which he liked to paint, but again and again it was made impossible for him to do so. Models would not pose for him and he was forbidden to paint in the street; with his irascible temper this caused many unpleasant scenes which excited him so much that he became completely unwanted to come back here, I would not hesitate for a moment . . . but again I think I can do no better than to let him follow his own inclinations . . . a quiet life is impossible for him, except alone with nature or with very simple people like the Roulins; for wherever he goes he leaves the trace of his passing. What ever he sees that is wrong he must criticize, and that often occasions strife.' (XLVIII)

Vincent expressed later in his letters his guilt for having created this upset at such an inconvenient time, and for interfering with the engagement and wedding arrangements. He bitterly regretted that Theo was called and reproached Gauguin for it; he similarly felt guilty about having occasioned so many extra expenses, like Theo's trip to Arles, hospital and doctor's fees, just at the time when Theo was in need of his money for his marriage. On the other hand, as we have already seen, he was soon to make more financial demands on Theo!

On January 7th he was allowed to return to the yellow house. Dr Rey's opinion at least at the beginning was that Vincent had suffered a temporary nervous collapse.

Nevertheless Vincent was still being troubled by insomnia and explained to Theo that before this crisis he was afraid to sleep alone in the yellow house and of not being able to sleep. He had not mentioned this symptom to the doctor and was trying to cure himself by placing a strong dose of camphor in his pillow and mattress, a procedure that he recommended to Theo (570). He described how during his illness his mind went back to the house at Zundert where he was born, and now he saw again 'every path, every plant in the garden, the views of the fields outside, the neighbours, the graveyard [where his older brother was buried], the church, our kitchen garden at the back – down to a magpie's nest in a tall acacia in the graveyard . . . There is no one left who remembers all this but mother and me'. (573) This statement shows clearly his phantasy of his unique communion with his mother.

He referred to having had hallucinations of an unbearable nature but did not describe them.

The hallucinations had ceased by the end of January when he stated, 'From what I am told, I am very obviously looking better, inwardly my heart is rather too full of so many feelings and divergent hopes, for I am amazed to be getting better' (513); instead he was having nightmares. He was being given bromide of potassium as a sedative. Before this crisis, while in Paris, he had suffered too from horrible nightmares that occurred regularly then and during which he suffered from fits of dizziness. They had disappeared soon after his arrival in Arles. In a letter to his sister W., he links them with an uneasy feeling about climbing stairs, and it is to be presumed that he suffered from a fear of heights. (W.4)

He warned his brother that he must not be considered completely sane and that other patients had told him the truth about their illnesses. He had little doubt that there would be other times when he would lose his head.

A turn of fate determined at this point that Vincent's best friend in Arles, the postman Roulin, should be removed to Marseilles to a new position. Roulin was an older man, a fatherly figure, benevolent and genuinely very fond of Vincent. He had been a great source of comfort to him before and during his illness. Vincent trusted Roulin and his family with whom he was always well received. He had painted several portraits of him, his wife (the several versions of La Berceuse) and some of his children. Roulin was to leave for Marseilles on January 21st, just at the point when Vincent was most in need of human warmth, of support, of some security and affection. Roulin's wife and the rest of the family moved away shortly afterwards too. This was a severe blow to Vincent. He was to say of him, 'Roulin though he is not quite old to be like a father to me, nevertheless has a silent gravity and a tenderness for me such as an old soldier might have for a young one. All the time – but without a word – a something which seems to say, We do not know what will happen to us tomorrow, but whatever it may be, think of me. And it does one good when it comes from a man who is neither embittered, nor sad, nor perfect, nor happy, nor always irreproachably just'. (583)

He described the scene of Roulin's departure in the two following beautiful paragraphs: 'Roulin left yesterday . . . It was touching to see him with his children this last day, especially with the quite tiny one, when he made her laugh and bounce on his knee, and sang for her.

'His voice has a strangely pure and touching quality in which there is to my ear at once a sweet and mournful lullaby and a kind of faraway echo of the trumpet of revolutionary France [Roulin was an ardent republican]. He was not sad, however. On the contrary, he had put on his brand new uniform which he had received that very day, and everyone was making a great deal of him.' (573)

This new separation from this very dear friend and fatherly figure at the worse possible of times, for somebody who was already seriously wounded by the effect of separations must have determined the fact that Vincent's mental equilibrium gave way again in the next few days. He was for the second time taken to hospital where he remained for only a few days.

Shortly after leaving the hospital, on February 9th he had to be taken back again. It is known that he now feared being poisoned. Once in hospital he did not utter a word for some time. On February 13th Dr Rey (Vincent's doctor) wired Theo that Vincent was much better and there was hope. A few days later Vincent wrote a reasonably normal letter asking his brother not to send him anywhere without his consent (sending him to Aix for further treatment had been considered); he argued that he wanted to stay at Arles where he had friends and liked Dr Rey. He added that he would rather always be ill at Arles than forget the kindness of the very people who have 'the most incredible prejudices against painters and painting'. (577) Soon afterwards he was allowed to return to the yellow house for a third time.

On February 24th he was sent to hospital again, this time without any cause, because of complaints made by a number of Arles citizens. The whole episode made a deep impression on Vincent and triggered off another attack from which according to Theo's wife, he recovered with astonishing speed. Vincent did not write until the middle of March when he excused himself for the delay; it was due to the 'fear of dragging you into it and upsetting you in what is before you' [Theo was about to get married]. (579) He explained in his letter that he was writing in full possession of his faculties and not as a madman. He had been taken to the sanatorium against his will because 80 neighbours had signed a petition describing him as unfit to be at liberty. Even his home had been sealed by the police. 'Anyhow here I am, shut up in a cell all the livelong day, under lock and key and with keepers, without my guilt being proved or even open to proof'. (579) He retained enough lucidity and control to understand that if he did not restrain his indignation, 'I should at once be thought a dangerous lunatic. Let us hope and have patience'. (579) He asked his brother nevertheless to leave things alone for the time being, to keep calm, and to leave him there until after his marriage when they could try to clear things up. He felt persecuted by people, a feeling that was on this occasion justified in reality by the behaviour of some of the Arlesiens. All he wanted was for people not to meddle with him when he was busy 'painting, or eating, or sleeping, or taking a turn at the brothel, since I haven't a wife'. (580) Arles was not too large a community and Vincent's attire and manner could not but incite some citizens to make fun of him and persecute him. The cutting of his ear, the incident at the brothel, etc., gave him further notoriety and in a small provincial town he became a kind of curiosity.

On March 18th, the Rev Mr Salles, a local Protestant minister whom Theo had asked to look after Vincent, wrote that Vincent was again perfectly lucid and calm but very grieved by the petition of the neighbours. 'If the police', he said to the Rev. Mr Salles, 'had protected my liberty by preventing the children and even the grown-ups from crowding around my house and climbing the windows as they have done (as if I were a curious animal), I should have more easily retained my self-possession; in any event I have done no harm to anyone.' (XLVII)

At the end of March he described the last three months as very strange to him. 'Sometimes moods of indescribable mental anguish, sometimes moments when the veil of time and the fatality of circumstances seemed to be torn apart for an instant.' (582) Around this time he was visited by the painter Signac who afterwards wrote to Theo that he found Vincent in good health physically and psychologically. They took walks together and Vincent had been allowed to go to the yellow house to show him his paintings.

At the beginning of April Vincent wrote that he was well 'except a certain undercurrent of vague sadness difficult to define'. (583) He said too that at times he suffered fits of atrocious remorse. He had started to work again but this undercurrent of depression was troublesome and ever present. In a letter to Paul Signac, who had just visited him, he wrote 'At times it is not easy for me to take up living again, for there remain inner seizures of despair of a pretty large calibre'. (583)

His reaction to and after Theo's wedding deserves particular attention. When he was about to be discharged from the hospital in Arles he decided he wanted to go and live in an institution; he suggested the hospital at St Remy that he had heard of. He wanted Theo to accept his decision without discussing the reasons for such a step, 'Talking about it would be mental torture'. (585) Nevertheless he explained that he was not able to tolerate the idea of being all on his own in a studio; he feared as well the neighbours' criticisms. The idea of living with another person was similarly frightening to him, 'I dare not even think of it'. (585) He concluded that being in an institution was the best for his own peace of mind and for that of others. In this way he was showing clearly the intensity of his inner turmoil, his fear of not being in control of his aggression, and of himself and consequently his need for the security provided by a protective environment. There was as well an unconscious wish to punish his brother with this decision because of the latter's marriage. Theo, of course, was distressed by Vincent's decision and general attitude.

In a letter to his sister W., written on April 10th, he told her that he was planning to go to the mental sanatorium at St Remy, a sanatorium that was run by nuns and priests, where he meant to stay for three months. He told her that in four months (between the end of December 1888 and April 1889) he had four crises – by which he meant acute episodes during which he did not know what he said, wanted or did. He added that previously he had had three fainting fits with no obvious cause about which he could remember nothing. He could not describe what seemed to be wrong with him but explained that 'now and then there are horrible fits of anxiety apparently without cause, or otherwise a feeling of emptiness and fatigue on the head'. (W.11) He adds that he takes every day Dickens's remedy against suicide – wine, bread, cheese and a pipe of tobacco, something he has mentioned earlier to his brother. He tells her that she 'will hardly be able to believe that this is the limit [suicide] to which melancholy will take me; all the same, at some moments – oh, oh dear me . . .' (W.11) Once he improved he was fully aware of how during the crisis he thought everything he imagined to be real. He described with great feeling the sadness of the last few days and his gratitude to

Theo: 'Certainly these last days were sad, with all the moving, taking away all my furniture, packing up the canvases that are going to you, but the thing I felt saddest about was that you had given me all these things with such brotherly love, and that for so many years you were always the one who supported me, and then to be obliged to come back and tell you this sorry tale – but it's difficult to express it as I felt it. The goodness you have shown me is not lost, because you had it and it remains for you; even if the material results should be nil, it remains for you all the more; I can't say it as I felt it'. (585)

There were other reasons for his wanting to go into the sanatorium. He considered this less expensive than keeping a house or a studio and being faced at the same time with all the outgoings involved in painting. He feared that because of it 'things might come to such a pitch that you would be short of money for your own housekeeping'. (589) He felt this would be appalling but he did not think that his paintings would be successful and sell. Why then waste this money? He was in a profoundly depressive mood and talked about Theo's kindness towards him and of his not being able to show any results in return. He felt very guilty because Theo had to continue to spend money and attention on him at the expense of his newly-acquired family. He advised his brother to 'transfer this affection to his wife as much as possible'. (585) He felt that his mind was not quite in order and warned Theo that he might not write 'very often because not all my days are clear enough for me to write fairly logically'. (585)

When he returned from hospital to the yellow house he found many of the paintings damaged by dampness and this further affected his depressive mood. He wrote, 'If I were without your friendship, they will remorselessly drive me to suicide, and however cowardly I am, I should end by doing it'. (588)

It is to be noted that there is little, if anything, in the letters from Arles during this period to betray the severity of Vincent's mental disturbance. One can identify his extreme sadness, despair and depression but the letters are coherent, logical, controlled. One can occasionally suspect a paranoid construction or delusion in a given sentence but these are perhaps easier to detect before this period. The paranoid delusions as such never found their way fully into the letters at this time. The letters remained generally well organized and constructed. It is of course possible that they were censored at the different mental institutions and that those showing obvious signs of disturbance were not allowed through. There are some indications that this was so at Arles but there remain those written in between hospitalizations which show no such signs either.

A similar phenomenon occurs with his paintings. One can point out certain changes in the style, in the handling of the brush strokes; there are signs in them of a certain urgency, a certain tension, of turmoil and even of violence, but his composition and perspective, his handling of colours and his colour scheme, etc., if slightly changed, do not in any noticeable way betray his mental derangement. It is true that frequently he was unable to paint during the worse part of the crises or was prevented from doing so by the hospital authorities. Yet he painted a great deal while disturbed without this showing in the finished work. Only his last work 'Crows in the Field' painted shortly before his suicide has signs of a loss of command and control; the composition and perspective are not right, according to Van Gogh's previous style, and there are two suns in the sky, but in spite of this the painting still makes a powerful impression.

At the beginning of May 1889 he settled at the asylum in St Remy. He wrote saying that the doctor there, Dr Peyron, considered that he suffers from some sort of epileptic attacks. He was to stay at St Remy for a whole year until the beginning of the second fortnight in May 1890 when he moved to Auvers-sur-Oise near Paris.

At St Remy he was reasonably well for some time and was allowed to go on painting excursions on his own. He smoked and drank now with frugality. On July 5th he received the news of her pregnancy from Theo's wife. They wanted to give the baby his name but he hesitated. No less important, Jo expressed her concern about Theo's health that for some time had been far from good. He tried to reassure her but was himself very preoccupied by it. Shortly after this news sometime during August he had another mental breakdown. He found it difficult to write because his head was so 'disordered'. He writes, 'For many days *my mind has been absolutely wandering*, as in Arles, quite as much if not worse'. (601) This attack distressed him much since he was starting to hope they would not come back, after three or four months of steady improvement.

Sometime in September Dr Peyron wrote to Theo informing him that Vincent had recovered from his crisis and had completely regained his lucidity of mind. He was back at painting as usual and his thoughts of suicide had disappeared; there remained a few symptoms including some disturbing dreams but even here there was improvement. During his lucid periods he was allowed a great deal of freedom and could visit the village at St Remy where he painted for example 'The Roadmenders'. At other times when he was unwell he was confined to his cell where he continued to paint, being allowed to go for walks only under strict supervision when some signs of improvement appeared.

It is known that during his stay at St Remy Vincent had wanted to kill himself and more than once had eaten some of his oil paints, some of which were quite poisonous. It is known as well that during some of the attacks he cried out incessantly, because he 'wanted to defend [himself] and could not do it' (588), but the nature of his delusions, or of the danger that made him feel so threatened and so defenceless, is not known.

On September 10th he wrote about the attacks, 'During the attack I feel a coward before the pain and suffering – more of a coward than I ought to be, and it is perhaps this very moral cowardice which whereas I had no desire to get better before, makes me eat like two now, work hard, limit my relations with the other patients for fear of relapse – altogether I am now trying to recover like a man who meant to commit suicide and finding the water too cold, tries to regain the bank'. (605) He explained to Theo that the attacks 'tend to take an absurd religious turn' and he thought that living in the old cloisters at St Remy with nuns and priests must be an unfavourable factor indicating the necessity of his return to the North. In the following letter a few days later he expressed his astonishment that in spite of his modern ideas he has 'attacks such as a superstitious man might have and that I get perverted and frightful ideas about religion such as never came into my head in the North'. (607) He wanted Theo to remove him quietly from St Remy if he developed 'another fit of religious exaltation again'. (607) He still had 'often terrible fits of depression' (611) coming over him but the 'abominable nightmares have stopped tormenting me'. (613)

Sometime during the end of November or the beginning of December he had another serious attack; he was overcome with discouragement though on this occasion the attack only lasted a week. Shortly before the following events took place. He had been exhibiting two paintings at the Independents, 'The Irises' and 'The Starlit Night'. That neither was sold was disappointing to him; on the other hand, according to Theo, the pictures had attracted attention and people talked to him about them occasionally. Vincent did not refer to his disappointment at this point but a few weeks later, when he was recovered from the earlier crisis and preparing for the next exhibition at the 'Vingstites' he wrote, 'If my health remains stable, then, if while I work I again start trying to sell, to exhibit, to make exchanges, perhaps I shall succeed a little in being less of a burden to you on the one hand and on the other may recover a little more zest'. (614)

Then there was the fact that Theo, whose health was steadily deteriorating was forced sometimes to write irregularly, and on top of this, he complained that he was seeing so many pictures that he would like to see none for a while. Though consciously Vincent could well understand Theo's meaning, unconsciously he may have been hurt by this, finding in it the confirmation of some of his worst expectations: a few weeks earlier he had said, 'Ah, now certainly you are you yourself deep in nature, since you say that Jo already feels her child move – it is much more interesting even than landscapes, and I am very glad that things should have changed so for you'. (611)

As we see, his fears of failure and of success were activated by all these events. His hopes of not being a burden to Theo any more were shattered. His fear that Theo's interest in his wife and the child yet to be born would distract him from paintings in general and from his own in particular found in his judgment some confirmation in the way described above. In reality Theo was trying hard to further his brother's interest.

Shortly afterwards there was to be the exhibition at the 'Vingstites' (the XX). He wrote to Vincent that they wanted some of his paintings for the XX at Brussels, explaining that among the other painters invited were Chavannes, Cezanne, Forain, Signac, L. Pissaro, Renoir, Sisley and Lautrec. To be invited was a considerable success in itself and Vincent who was already ill when the letter arrived, was asked by Dr Peyron if he wanted to exhibit. He answered that he did not want to exhibit anything. When he recovered soon afterwards he regretted this and fortunately there was still time to send the pictures for the exhibition. This exhibition was to prove later on to have been a turning point in terms of Vincent's artistic success.

Finally he went to Arles for two days on a visit; this was taken to be a test of his ability to leave St Remy and live somewhere else, perhaps near Theo. Vincent, though he wanted to leave St Remy, was unsure and frightened of doing so and failed the test. All these stresses and what they reactivated proved too much for him and he developed yet another crisis.

While at St Remy he had started to copy paintings by other artists in his own personal style because at times, when he was too disturbed, his movements had to be restricted and he lacked subjects to paint from nature. He had pangs of conscience because of this and was afraid that he would be accused of plagiarizing. It is of special interest to note that at this point he was unable to copy a painting of the Virgin, I believe by Millet, because he found the Virgin so dazzling that did not dare to look at her. He wrote 'My illness makes me very sensitive now and for the moment I do not feel capable of continuing these "translations" when it concerns such masterpieces'. (625)

On February 24th Dr Peyron told Theo that Vincent was again ill after having returned to Arles for two days. The attack had started there and nobody knew where he had spent the previous evening. Furthermore he had taken a picture of an Arlesienne with him which was lost and has never been found. He was brought back to St Remy in a carriage. This attack lasted longer than some of the others and in April he was still far from well. A number of interesting factors that preceded this new attack deserve consideration.

He had gone to Arles from St Remy and may have visited the Ginoux family. He had done some portraits of Mme Ginoux (L'Arlesienne), who also suffered from severe emotional disturbances and nervousness. In a later letter (634a) to her husband he regretted haven fallen ill the day he went to Arles to say good-bye to them all.

Aurier's article about Vincent's work had just been published in the *Mercure de France*. Vincent read it at the very end of January 1890. It was full of praise and compliments. Vincent was partly pleased and partly disturbed by it. He felt he did not deserve this praise and went so far as to write to Aurier saying that he should write about Gauguin (about father) and not about him. We know that he dreaded having his work praised. He had earlier begged Isaacson (another art critic and painter) not to write about his work because it would make him very sad. This attitude related, as we have discussed in detail already, to his insurmountable fear of success and failure.

Vincent's unconscious hostility towards Jo and her son yet to be born found expression on a conscious level towards the end of her pregnancy in the form of a tormenting preoccupation about her safety and that of the baby. He referred repeatedly to this in different letters. To Jo herself he wrote, 'How I am longing to get the news that you have come safely through, and that your child is living'. (624) On February 1st he received the news that the baby was born and all was well. Consciously he was pleased and relieved, but the dreaded rival had finally arrived safely. From his letters it is possible to reconstruct the following sequence, which is of great significance in respect of the tensions that may have led to the new crisis. On February 15th he wrote to his mother stating that he would have preferred Theo's child to be called not Vincent after himself, but Theo in memory of their father. It was, after all, his brother's name as well. He continued saying that he started 'a picture for him, to hang in their bedroom, big branches of white almond blossom against blue sky'. (622) It is not surprising that it was while working at this painting for his nephew that he first felt ill again. He wrote 'I felt ill at the time I was doing the almond blossoms' (629), and 'My work was going well, the last canvas of branches in blossom – you will see that it was perhaps the best, the most patiently worked thing I had done, painted with calm and with a greater firmness of touch. And then the next day, down like a brute'. (628)

In some ways this child was like a reincarnation of the dead brother whose absence-presence had haunted him all his life. And the boy was named Vincent like his brother, and himself. The first one was dead, the second mad; thus the name was a bad omen. For the child to have this name of his dead brother must have increased his anxiety over his unconscious death wishes against it. This did not show directly but appeared in the form of a reaction formation, that is, as an intense preoccupation for the health of the child and extreme anxiety when the child became ill. Added to all this, to have given the boy his name and not that of the boy's grand-

12. THE YELLOW CHAIR

This meaningful painting represents Vincent's own chair at Arles. It is very plain and rustic as suits his character. It is to be contrasted with the armchair he acquired for Gauguin, luxurious and refined. Empty chairs are generally associated with absent or dead persons and that was particularly so in Vincent's case. (See Chapter 16, The Two Empty Chairs, page 137.) Most of the objects in the painting were unconsciously selected by their symbolic meaning. The whole drama of his father's death, his attack on Gauguin and his own future suicide are represented in this canvas. (See Chapter 16, The Two Empty Chairs, pages 132–42, where the symbolic meaning of the two paintings is discussed in detail.)

Photo by courtesy of the Trustees of the Tate Gallery, London

13. GAUGUIN'S ARMCHAIR

This painting seems to express the best for Gauguin, the 'master and poet'. Indeed, Vincent bought for Gauguin a rich, refined and rather feminine armchair while he was contented with a plain and rustic one (See The Yellow Chair.) The rich symbolic content of the painting is described in Chapter 16, The Two Empty Chairs, page 132.

Photo by courtesy of the Amsterdam Municipal Museum

father was an offence to his dead father's memory and we know that he had been thinking a great deal about his father at some points during his illness. Thus it is not surprising that he himself traced the beginning of the crisis to the picture he was painting for his nephew, though he may not have been fully aware of the implications of this link. Clearly, the positive aspects of his ambivalence towards the child, the only ones allowed into his conscious mind, gave him not only the idea of making the picture for his nephew's room but led him to try his best in this picture; as he said it was the most patiently worked thing he had done. The negative aspects of the ambivalence – of which he had little if any conscious awareness – created a situation of tension and conflict that was much reinforced by the other elements referred to above. They led to a new and prolonged attack of insanity. This was the fifth acute psychotic episode he had suffered in little more than a year.

By May it was decided that he was to leave for Auvers-sur-Oise. He refused to be accompanied during the railway journey in case of an attack as had been suggested, because he was 'not one of those who are dangerous'. (631)

Vincent finally arrived in Paris towards the second fortnight of May, 1890. He was met by his brother who was anxiously waiting for him at the railway station. He stayed only a few days in Paris with his brother, meeting his sister-in-law and his nephew. Jo described the scene of the first meeting with the baby as follows: 'Silently the two brothers looked at the quietly sleeping baby – both had tears in their eyes. Then Vincent turned smiling to me and said, pointing to the simple crocheted cover on the cradle, "Do not cover him too much with lace, little sister".' (4)

At Auvers-sur-Oise he met Dr Gachet who was to look after him and he took a room at a cafe-restaurant. Dr Gachet, who lived at Auvers, was not a psychiatrist but a cardiologist with a practice in Paris. He used to go several days a week to Paris for consultations. He was himself an amateur artist signing his work with the pseudonym Van Rijssel, and counted among his friends Cezanne, Guillaumin Pisarro, Sisley, Renoir, Monet and others, many of whom were Vincent's friends as well. He owned a valuable collection of paintings by several of these artists, now to be seen at the Louvre Museum. Everybody hoped that Vincent would improve, thanks to the friendly atmosphere of Auvers, the

I

nearness to his family in Paris, and the gentle and sympathetic supervision of Gachet.

Gachet gave Vincent the by no means incorrect impression of being rather eccentric. He thought that 'his experience as a doctor must keep him balanced enough to combat the nervous trouble from which he certainly seems to me to be suffering at least as seriously as I'. (635) In any case Vincent threw himself into his work and painted some of his most beautiful pictures during this period.

On June 10th he was feeling better and wrote that his nightmares hardly ever recurred now; he had always thought that coming back to the North would free him from them.

There remain some factors of a rather different nature which are deserving of mention, since his illness at Arles was originally attributed to them. Among them were included Vincent's consumption of alcohol. He had been a very heavy drinker by all accounts including those of Vincent himself. Although he had started drinking earlier it was in Paris that he did so heavily and from then onwards he drank more or less continuously.

The painter Signac who knew Vincent well expressed the following opinion to a friend: 'Never did he give me the impression of being a mad man. Though he ate hardly anything, what he drank was always too much. Returning after spending the whole day in the blazing sun, in the torrid heat, and having no real home in town, he would take his seat on the terrace of a cafe. And the absinthes and brandies would follow each other in quick succession. How was it possible to resist? He hardly took any food. He was charm personified. He loved life passionately. He was ardent and good.' It should be noted that Signac was close to Van Gogh only before the time of his serious breakdown at Arles, when he visited him only once at a point when Vincent was in a period of remission between two crises. Furthermore as is frequently the case with heavy drinkers,[1] Vincent ate too little, smoked a great deal and drank a lot of coffee. The physician at St Remy, Dr Peyron, seems to have thought, at least for some time, that this abuse of his constitution, associated with the intense work at his paintings, had provoked his nervous collapse. He expressed the opinion that a more hygienic and regimented system should go a long way towards returning his health. He obviously underestimated the disturbance, though it seems reasonable to assume

[1] Vincent drank a great deal of absinthe, a particularly toxic drink.

that all these factors may have created a very weakened background for the internal and external stresses he was to be subjected to.

Dr Peyron visited Theo on one occasion in Paris and seems to have stated that Vincent was not a 'lunatic' but that his crises were of an epileptic nature. Vincent commented to his sister, 'Consequently alcohol is also not the cause, though it must be understood that it does me no good either.' (W.15)

Many other opinions have been expressed, including the possibility of schizophrenia, but all these attempts at fitting him into a given diagnostic category are rather unconvincing and unsatisfactory. His nephew, the engineer Van Gogh, concurs with the opinion expressed by Professor Kraus that Vincent's morbid condition might perhaps be best characterized in a vague descriptive way as 'psychogenic attacks on a psychopathic basis'. He remarks, rightly I think, that Vincent was in his art as well as in his 'illness' an individualist. One cannot help having some sympathy for this view, if by 'psychopathic' he implies, as I presume, a neurotic basis on which psychotic-like episodes were triggered off by psychological stresses.

≈ 16 ≈

THE TWO EMPTY CHAIRS

AROUND Christmas 1888 Vincent painted two pictures each one representing an empty chair. The study of these two paintings from the psychoanalytic point of view is a most rewarding exercise.

One of them was Vincent's own chair at Arles, the other Gauguin's. The Empty Chair (Vincent's chair or the yellow chair as it is usually called), is now in the collection of the Tate Gallery in London. Gauguin's chair was in the private collection of the engineer V. W. Van Gogh in Holland.[1] A superficial examination of the the chairs shows Vincent's to be very simple, rustic, without arms, painted in yellow against a background of ordinary bare red tiles. We can observe in the background a wall, the door and, towards the left hand corner, a box with onions. Vincent's signature appears on the box, a peculiarity that is to be observed in some other paintings of his as well. Placed on the chair in a prominent place is his pipe and by its side some tobacco. Gauguin's chair is totally different from Vincent's. It is a much more refined chair with arms, more feminine in character. The background too is very different; there is a carpet on the floor instead of the rustic red tiles, the wall behind is deep green in colour and there

[1] Specific references to these pictures by Vincent Van Gogh are to be found in Letters 563, 571 and 626a.

The collection of the engineer Van Gogh is now in the possession of the Vincent Van Gogh Foundation. He informs me that the Netherlands government is building in Amsterdam the Vincent Van Gogh Museum, where the collection will be housed. He further called my attention, after reading this manuscript, to a paper in The American Imago, 1956, No. 3, by Dr Harold P. Blum entitled 'Van Gogh's Chairs'. The reader may be interested to see how two analysts working independently on the same material (Vincent's letters) have arrived at very similar inferences and conclusions.

is a light burning on it. On the chair a candle is burning, and by its side are some novels, modern novels according to Vincent's own description. Vincent's chair, one may add, is painted in the light of day in his own very personal style. Gauguin's chair represents a night scene and shows a strong influence of Gauguin's style. Taken at face value the two paintings do not tell us a great deal, yet they are rich in psychological content, the carriers of many important unconscious messages. To penetrate these secrets we must see them against their appropriate background.

Vincent bought Gauguin's chair shortly before the latter's arrival at Arles. Vincent had been on his own for some months feeling very lonely, when he heard from Theo that Gauguin, then in Pont Aven, was in difficult financial circumstances and had asked him for help. Vincent greatly admired Gauguin as a painter and considered him 'the painter of the future'. Furthermore Gauguin was a powerful father figure in Vincent's unconscious. He immediately conceived the idea of having Gauguin come down to Arles to live with him. He thought that with his allowance, or just a little more, he and Gauguin could live together under the same roof. He told his brother that he did not think he could afford to keep Gauguin in Pont Aven and himself in Arles, but that for Gauguin to come to Arles could be the solution to everybody's problems. At Vincent's suggestion they made the offer to Gauguin who did not refuse outright but hesitated for over six months before finally coming down to Arles.

Gauguin's hesitation is in no way surprising. Vincent was known to be difficult and Arles was in the middle of nowhere. At Pont Aven there was a colony of artists of which he was the acknowledged leader, and he was near Paris. Arles meant giving all this up for isolation. It meant moving farther away from his family, a matter that was perhaps in the last extreme not of great concern to him. He held fast to Pont Aven for as long as he could, but his paintings were not selling and he had too many creditors. There was the further fact that Theo was an important art dealer who liked his paintings very much and could promote their sale. In all fairness to Theo's memory it must be said that he would not have dreamed of putting pressure on Gauguin to go to Arles, much as he wanted some company for Vincent, but Gauguin had a cold, calculating mind and he must have drawn certain conclusions.

In the meantime Vincent's anxiety about Gauguin's decision

increased. He suspected that Gauguin would not come if he had any other alternative open to him. For months he continued to be concerned with this problem as we have already seen. In one letter he suggested to Theo that they withdraw the offer to Gauguin, in the next the offer was to be reiterated and they were to be patient with him. Another letter was to state that he did not really mind if Gauguin did not come, somebody else would do so in the end, and he was not really lonely; the following one would remark on his need for Gauguin's company and his loneliness. If Gauguin could not come South he would go North to him. Gauguin only had to say the word and he would go, perhaps this was after all the better solution.

On the other hand he continued to make plans for Gauguin's arrival. If Gauguin came this could be the beginning of a community of painters in the house of friends. As in a religious community they would have an Abbot and who but Gauguin was best suited for this position?

Vincent wrote to his brother that the association with Gauguin could only increase his own and Theo's prestige. His conviction that Gauguin was the 'painter of the future' and that he would rise to great fame must have led to phantasies that through their working together he too would achieve success and fame; and, since his own pictures did not sell, the sales of Gauguin's paintings would alleviate Theo's economic burdens. There was on the other hand a genuine desire on his side to help the talented fellow painter. He wrote, 'I thought he was on the rocks, and there I was with money, and this boy who does better work than I do with none, so I said he ought to have half of mine'. (498)

He started to decorate and prepare Gauguin's room even before there was any certainty that Gauguin would come. Interestingly enough, he started to decorate the room Gauguin was to occupy as if it were for a woman; he wanted it to be like a beautiful boudoir. He wrote to his brother, 'For a visitor there will be the prettier room upstairs, which I shall try to make as much as possible like the boudoir of a really artistic woman . . . the sunflowers, 12 or 14 to the bunch, crammed into this tiny boudoir with its pretty bed and everything else dainty'. (534) Such a room was of course more suitable for a mistress than for the very virile and masculine Gauguin. This curious behaviour on Vincent's part becomes understandable if we take into account again the intensity of his bisexual conflicts and of his unconscious passive-feminine longings and phantasies. They were stirred up by the possibility of living with Gauguin as has happened earlier when he went to live with Theo in Paris. His automatic defence against them was to turn Gauguin in his unconscious into a woman, thus attempting to solve the problem posed by his homosexual longings. Further, he expected Gauguin to take a feminine role in the household and to do the cooking for both of them. Already we can understand some of the reasons for the striking differences between Vincent's chair and Gauguin's and the different backgrounds of each painting particularly the rather feminine quality of that of Gauguin's chair and its prettier surroundings.

Gauguin finally arrived in Arles on October 20, 1888, and the two friends started living and working together. As we have explained earlier it was in the nature of things that these two strong artistic personalities had to clash. Gauguin was used to being the leader and Vincent could not be a follower: such a position could only increase his fear of his passivity. Because of this same conscious fear of being (and unconscious wish to be) completely influenced and dominated by Gauguin's personality we have already seen him working hard to show Gauguin, that he had an individuality of his own. He hoped 'father' Gauguin would acknowledge it and show some small appreciation of his art, just as he had tried hard in the past to have his father acknowledge his individuality and to show some appreciation of his paintings. I have explained earlier as well that both painters were the holders of highly original views about art that in many cases did not run parallel and that both were given to expressing their opinions strongly. Soon they were quarrelling violently much of the time. Gauguin was obviously unhappy and wrote to Theo that he would leave Arles since they were quite incompatible. Vincent managed to persuade him to stay and Gauguin wrote again to Theo explaining that he would do so after all; the whole thing had been like a bad dream but it was now over. But the nightmare was far from over, they continued to argue and Vincent grew more and more restless and disturbed. There were many reasons for his increased distress apart from his massive conflicts with his unconscious homosexual strivings in relation to Gauguin. Gauguin was very masculine and virile, and very successful with the Arlesiennes. Vincent was not at all successful with them, furthermore his potency was already failing. Moreover Vincent was affected by the fact that things had begun to change for Gauguin. He had started to have some success. Theo had managed to sell three of his paintings while Vincent's did not sell. Theo had a genuine admiration for Gauguin's art as Vincent did, but the latter could not help reacting with some jealousy, especially when his brother praised Gauguin. As had happened in the past, for example when Theo had praised De Haan's and Isaäcson's work, he reproached himself, stating in a letter that he could not help it if his paintings did not sell but he would do still better things and perhaps then buyers would be attracted. Gauguin because of this success started talking about leaving sometime in the future to fulfil his dream of going to the tropics again, 'He intends to save money when he sells, till the time (say in a year) when he has enough to risk a second voyage to Martinique'. (559) The idea of Gauguin going away, leaving him, abandoning him, touched old and very painful areas of his personality. He became more disturbed and quarrelsome. He wrote, 'Our arguments are terribly electric, sometimes we come out of them with our heads as exhausted as a used electric battery'. (564)

He suspected Gauguin of wanting to leave not in the future but at any moment and though greatly distressed he wrote to Theo that he awaited Gauguin's decision with all serenity. Just before Christmas, and before attempting to attack Gauguin with a razor, he painted his own empty chair and Gauguin's empty chair, thus expressing on canvas the drama that was to develop in no more than a few hours. Unconsciously he had passed a death sentence on them both hence the empty chairs. In the letter to Theo in which he announced the painting of these two pictures he remarked himself on the oddity of the subjects, 'I can at all events tell you that the last two studies are odd enough'. (563) Shortly afterwards, as we have described, he followed Gauguin into the street armed with a razor but did not complete the attack; he turned round and ran away when Gauguin noticed him. We know that he went back to the yellow house, where, turning the hostility he felt towards Gauguin against himself, he cut his ear lobe and in a fit of madness took it to the brothel, well wrapped, as a present for Rachel the prostitute. After returning to the yellow house he was taken to the mental hospital in Arles where he remained feverish and delirious for several days.

To understand this action properly we must search in Vincent's past for its underlying motivations. His fear of loneliness and extreme reaction to feeling rejected, abandoned and unwanted we know of from his accusations of his family and above all of his father. In Vincent's unconscious Gauguin played among other roles first and foremost that of a substitute father figure (he was as well a brother substitute, a mother and a wife). Gauguin's rejection and assumed imminent departure reactivated all the conflicts and the accompanying hostility to his father with which we are already familiar. Furthermore Vincent had a deeply seated fear of separation that we first noticed in his reaction to his father's departure when he was taken as a boarder to a school away from home. He was overwhelmed then and watched the carriage in which the parents left for as long as he could see it. We know similarly, how when he was forced to leave home for The Hague at sixteen to become an art dealer he took every possible opportunity at week-ends and holidays to return home. Though being away from his family brought him to his knees, he tried as hard as he could to cope with these feelings out of his strong desire to please his father. When he was transferred to London at the age of twenty, without the possibility of frequent trips home for comfort and reassurance, his mental equilibrium finally gave way, and after the Ursula incident we found a completely changed man. He was depressed and a massive anal regression had taken place that transformed him from a pleasant and promising employee at the house of Goupil into one whom they were forced to dismiss for his rudeness and lack of tact with clients. Clearly the present incident had reactivated all these conflicts and provoked a catastrophic reaction.

That an 'empty chair' was a death symbol for Vincent finds confirmation in the following episodes of his life and passages from his letters. He had once, many years earlier, seen a drawing of an 'empty chair' by Fildes that greatly impressed him, though the reasons for this were of course unknown to him. He so admired this drawing that he spent a great deal of his free time looking for a reproduction of it in second-hand shops, etc., to send to his friend Rappard to whom he had written several times about this drawing. He could not in the end find a reproduction. That his intense interest in this drawing was determined by its being for him a symbolic representation of death becomes apparent in a letter he wrote to his brother during the Hague period. He was referring to how Fildes went to see Dickens with the purpose of illustrating his latest work, *Edwin Drood*. Dickens was then very ill and Fildes 'entered his room on the day of his death and so it happened that one of the old numbers of the Graphic contained that touching drawing "The Empty Chair".' (252) He further commented on how there were already many 'empty chairs' and how more would become vacant as some old contemporary artists died. He said: 'Empty chairs – there are many of them, there will be even more, and sooner or later there will be nothing but empty chairs in place of Herkomet, Luke Fildes, Frank Holl, William Small, etc.' (252) The conscious link here with death is quite clear. At home too there had always been an empty chair, that of his dead elder brother. There is nevertheless an even more significative link. During the Amsterdam period (1877-8) while Vincent was studying in order to become a parson, his father came to visit him. He frequently thought back with great pleasure to the moments they spent togehter in his little room, his father correcting some of his work and talking generally. The scene when his father had to depart was highly reminiscent of the one when his father went away after leaving him behind at boarding school, and it seems that on this later occasion similar feelings were aroused. He had gone to see his father off at the station, and had looked after the train for as long as it was in sight 'even the smoke from it – then I came home to my room and saw father's chair still standing near the little table on which the books and copy books of the day before were still lying, though I know that we shall see each other again pretty soon, I cried like a child'. (118) Vincent was twenty-five years of age at this time. From his description of his reaction to seeing the empty chair where his father had been sitting we can conclude that for an instant he behaved as if his father had died, or was about to die, and as if he would never see him again. His father's departure must have reactivated the hostility and death wishes aroused by being left by him at school, away from home, many years earlier. The reader will have noticed that reference to the books he and his father have been looking at together. They appear as an important element on Gauguin's empty chair by the side of the burning candle, itself a symbol not only of Gauguin's virility, in contrast to his own impotency, but also of Gauguin's death as well as that of his father.

The reaction to Gauguin's possible departure can now be better understood. His attack on Gauguin is a break-through into actual behaviour of his hostility and death wishes against his father now reinforced by his hostility towards Theo and towards Gauguin himself. To further understand the pictures and the elements depicted on them we must remind ourselves of some of the episodes that took place during the Nuenen period (1883–5) preceding the death of his father. By that time the original idealization, near adoration, Vincent felt for his father had transformed itself as we have seen into quite open hostility and aggression. The father reacted to Vincent's hostility by telling him repeatedly that 'he was killing him' with his behaviour and unjust accusations. He even wrote to his son Theo accusing Vincent in similar terms. Vincent became more incensed by such accusations and flatly rejected them. These were very difficult times indeed in the relationship between father and son. Fate was now to play its hand: the Reverend Van Gogh collapsed and died at the front door of his house on his return from an errand. His sudden death had been preceded by weeks of intense quarrelling and accusations. In this context, Vincent's reaction to his father's death was of marked interest. From having constantly, in every letter to Theo, referred to his father at length in the most open aggressive and derogatory manner he made no further reference to him after his death apart from a very few exceptions. Thus, he described the father's death in the following terms, 'the total impression was not terrible, only solemn'. (397) In the same letter he says that he too (like Theo) had been apathetic after the father's death for a few days but was already back at work. There is no sign in the letters of any conscious guilt or remorse in spite of the traumatic circumstances of his father's death and of the many quarrels and accusations that preceded it. Nevertheless he painted a commemorative picture, a blue vase with flowers on a table; by the side of the vase and towards the front lie his father's pipe and tobacco pouch. He sent the painting to Theo for him to see it and keep if he so wished. We can of course recognize in the picture of his own empty chair the two elements of the pipe and the tobacco lying on the chair. They represent in symbolic terms his father's death, but they are now his own pipe and tobacco lying on his own empty chair as a clear indication of his own death through the 'talion law'[1] of the unconscious; these

[1] Talion law: 'an eye for an eye'.

objects point as well to the crime he has symbolically committed.

Now he felt the full impact of his father's death and of his 'responsibility' in bringing it about. The attack on Gauguin (in so far as he represented the father) constituted a re-enactment of the whole complex of Vincent's father's death years earlier, when he seemed to have successfully repressed any feelings of guilt. The association of events and multiple factors in his present life that led to the attack reactivated all sorts of earlier conflicts belonging to the relationship to his father. There is just one important difference: on this occasion the impulse to kill *did* break through into his conscious mind and *was* acted upon, though in the last instance he managed to turn it away from Gauguin and against himself. This is in sharp contrast to the situation at the time of his father's death when such impulses, undoubtedly present in his unconscious phantasies, were able to find expression only through provocative behaviour and verbal abuse of his father. In Gauguin's 'empty chair' are thus condensed the conscious murderous intentions towards Gauguin and the unconscious wishes to kill the father – but these impulses have now been acted upon. Vincent has thus in symbolic terms committed the oedipal crime. Such a crime cannot go without punishment and so his own chair is painted at the same time as that of Gauguin. His chair is empty too, symbolizing his own death; his pipe and his tobacco lie on the empty chair, just as his father's pipe and tobacco pouch appear in the picture that commemorated his death.

Vincent must die, and die he will through his own hand not long after this incident. But before that final act is played he dies symbolically through becoming deranged. Such symbolic death postpones for a short while his actual physical death. It is necessary at this point to recall The Hague period. It was then that Theo suggested to him that the family (Vincent took this to mean his father) was considering having him placed under guardianship in a mental institution. They thought him unfit to manage his affairs because of his abnormal behaviour and his association with Sien the prostitute. He reacted then by warning Theo that he would not take this passively, uttering a veiled threat that in such circumstances one could even kill the offenders (in this case his father) and get acquitted by the law as had happened in the example he quoted. Yet in losing his reason and by being institutionalized he was complying with what he thought to be his father's wishes. The father was right after all, he was mad and dangerous. He should be under care, especially after the attack on Gauguin. He was imposing on himself the punishment he thought the father had ready for him when he rebelled against his authority. Further we have seen how he decided freely, during a lucid interval, that it would be best for himself and others for him to live in a mental institution for some time. This in fact he did by going to St Remy. Finally, we should point out that from the time Vincent cut his ear lobe onwards there is a significative change in his signature, pointing to the symbolic self-castration (another unconscious equivalent of his death) that he has just carried out. His paintings were usually signed, if at all, with his Christian name, but the initial 'V' was a character with a very sharp angle. This 'V' was now with only a few exceptions changed into a rounded '*V*', all sharpness disappearing from it. This change had already started to appear occasionally after Gauguin's arrival in Arles – and is to be noted in the picture of his own empty chair – but it became a permanent feature of his signature at this point.

The richness in psychological content of these two paintings, so completely representational in character, may be surprising to some. Many will have noticed that I have treated them somewhat as if they were the manifest content of a patient's dream.

In the case of the analysis of a dream it is through the agency of the patient's free associations to it that we usually arrive at its latent content, its hidden meaning. In this case I have substituted for the lack of such free associations a search into the events around the time when the pictures were painted, and extended the search with the help of my general knowledge of the significant circumstances in the life of the painter, through those associative paths linking with the episodes that find conscious expression in the pictures. I have thus reconstructed what might have been Vincent's own associations.

The complexity of psychological phenomena condensed in each painting will not seem strange to anyone who is familiar with the working of unconscious mental processes, the process of condensation and the principle of multiple determination.

It is now possible to understand some of the reasons for the dramatic impact of these paintings of the empty chairs. Though one can identify the early origins of the feelings expressed on the

VINCENT VAN GOGH

canvas, the means by which Van Gogh succeeded in expressing
them, in embodying them on the canvas, in conveying them to
the casual observer, remains to this day the secret of his genius
and the testimony of it.

VINCENT'S CONFLICTS AROUND SEXUALITY – THEIR INFLUENCE ON HIS PAINTING

VINCENT'S attitude to sexuality deserves examination. We find a number of references to it in his letters to Theo but he wrote more freely in this respect to his friend, the painter and poet Emile Bernard. Bernard was very young, the Benjamin of this group of painters, and Vincent occasionally took with him the liberty of a slightly patronizing paternal attitude. Vincent's sexual experiences were largely confined to contacts with prostitutes. As he said, he had 'hardly seen anything but the kind of women at 2 francs, originally intended for the Zouaves [soldiers]'. (522) He had the impression, communicated to Bernard in June 1888, that 'painting and fucking a lot are not compatible; it weakens the brain which is a bloody nuisance'. (B.7) Similarly he said to Theo, 'What Gruby [a physician they used to consult in Paris] says about doing without women and eating well is true, for if your brain and marrow are going into your work, it is pretty sensible not to exhaust yourself more than you must in love making'. (521)

He advises young Bernard to live like a monk, but to go to a brothel once a fortnight. This is what he does himself, 'it's not very poetic, but I feel it my duty after all to subordinate my life to painting'. (B.8)

He frequently comes back in his letters to this argument that painting and an active sexual life are not quite compatible. It drains the brain and the creative sap of the artist. He writes in August 1888 to Bernard, 'Personally I feel that continence is good for me, that it is enough for our weak, impressionable artists' brain to give their essence to the creation of our pictures . . . Why exert ourselves to pour out all our creative sap where the well-fed professional pimps and ordinary fools do better in the matter of satisfying the genital organs of the whore'. (B.14)

He discusses with Bernard the painter Degas who is said not to like women. 'He knows that if he loved them and fucked them often, he, intellectually diseased, would become insipid as a painter.' (B.14) He thinks that Degas is contented with seeing and painting the human animals who 'get excited and fuck'. He thinks he paints them well 'exactly because he doesn't have the pretention to get excited himself'. (B.14) He quotes Balzac who 'has told us that relative chastity fortifies the modern artist'. (B.14) Delacroix 'did not fuck much, and only had easy love affairs, so as not to curtail the time devoted to his work'. (B.14) He concludes that he and Bernard, if they really want to be potent males in [their] work, must 'resign ourselves to not fuck much, and for the rest be monks or soldiers, according to the needs of our temperament'. (B.14)

He thinks there are some exceptions to these rules in the case of very healthy natures – like Courbet, and Rubens whom he describes as 'handsome and a good fucker'.

Later on he was to express a similar opinion of Gauguin, describing him as a kind of savage in whom blood and sex came first. Whilst at Arles he felt extremely jealous of Gauguin's virility and success with the Arlesiennes. It was a direct reminder of his own potency difficulties. To his sister W. he wrote, 'I am so fond of my friend Gauguin because he has found the means of producing children and pictures at the same time'. (W.19) He envied his ability to be sexually free and to produce children without any noticeable impairment of his ability to paint. For him these were incompatible alternatives and he had decided – perhaps forced by circumstances – for painting at the expense and sacrifice of everything else including the possibility of a family of his own.

When he rented the 'yellow house' at Arles he played with the idea of tempting a 'little woman' to come and live with him but he thought that 'with [his] disposition going on a spree and working are not at all compatible and in the present circumstances one must content oneself with painting pictures. It is not really living at all, but what is one to do? And indeed, this artistic life, which we know is not *the* real life, seems to me so vital, one would be ungrateful not to be content with it'. (480) Sometime earlier he had written of himself, 'I feel I am losing the desire for marriage and children, and now and then it saddens me that I should be feeling like that at thirty-five, just when it should be the opposite. And sometimes I have a grudge against this rotten painting. It was Richepin who said somewhere: "The love of art makes one lose real love".' (462)

He concludes in a letter to his brother, 'If we want to live and work, we must be very sensible and look after ourselves. Cold water, fresh air, simple food, decent clothes, a decent bed and no women. And not to let oneself go with women, or with life that is life, as much as one would like to'. (481) At around this time he shows indirectly some concern about his potency while talking about Braekeleer. He wrote to Theo, 'Have you heard that he suffered from a disease of the brain which left him impotent??? I have heard this, but wasn't it only temporary?' (482)

After one of Theo's illnesses he thinks the doctor will make Theo 'promise to have nothing to do with women except in case of necessity, but anyhow as little as possible'. (489)

After he had been for sometime in Arles he had difficulties with his potency. He introduces this subject in a letter to his brother by reminding him of a character in one of Guy de Maupassant's novels 'who had hunted [rabbits and other game] so hard for ten years, and was so exhausted by running after the game that when he wanted to get married he found he was impotent, which caused the greatest embarrassment and consternation'. He confesses that though he has no desire to get married he is beginning to resemble this man physically. He further remarks that 'according to the worthy Zien, man becomes ambitious as soon as he becomes impotent. Now though it is pretty much the same to me whether I'm impotent or not, I'm damned if that's going to drive me to ambition'. (506)

The above passage is very illuminating from another point of view, that of Vincent's unconscious equation between painting and masturbation. The magnitude of his conflicts around masturbation can be inferred from the fact that athough he was a man of strong passions he did not come to have regular intercourse with a woman until he met Sien in The Hague, by which time he was already twenty-nine years old.

Unconsciously he seems to think that it is masturbation that has ruined him as a man, ruined his mind and his ability to create a family as well as his sexual potency. Painting is an attempt at sublimation of his masturbation conflicts and sexuality generally, and at the same time a substitute and a symbol for them. Maupassant's character had exhausted himself, becoming impotent through the rentless pursuit of hunting rabbits – a symbolic description of his having exhausted his potency through masturbation – becoming useless for married life. Several weeks later in another letter the link with Vincent himself is made more apparent. He refers to how in the old days he felt less of a painter (presumably when he was living with Sien and had more of a sexual life) but now (in Arles) painting is becoming a distraction for him 'like rabbit hunting for the cracked brained [i.e. masturbation]: they do it to distract themselves'. (513) His concentration has improved and his hand is more sure as the result of taking on painting. He naturally concludes, 'that is why I almost dare to swear to you that my painting will improve. Because I have nothing left but that'. (513) Painting for him is thus a substitute for masturbation, a step in the direction of the sublimation of his sexual impulses. Painting is a particular suitable vehicle for Vincent because it can embody the essential components of his sexuality, not only his phallic creative strivings but also the strong anal components with which in his case they are contaminated. The media of oil painting form a traditionally well-known outlet for the gratification of otherwise forbidden anal impulses. The consistency, the strong smells, the messiness are highly enjoyable for the anal personality and allow for the non-conflictive gratification of the impulses to touch (the faeces), to enjoy the strong and diverse smells, to mess, etc. Such tendencies were particularly marked in Vincent who used his hands as a brush quite freely in order to create particular effects. These habits of his led to serious arguments with his relative and teacher Mauve who could tolerate neither Vincent's messiness and dirtiness nor his constantly touching the canvas with his fingers.

Vincent firmly believed that painting (as a symbol of masturbation) had ruined him as a man making him useless for love, for family life, and for the procreation of children. It had drained away all energy and rendered him quite incapable of anything else. Furthermore, especially during the Arles period, he painted as in a day-dream, and his feelings while painting are, as he describes them, very close indeed to intense orgastic experiences that leave him exhausted and tired. This is best expressed by

Vincent himself when he refers to how a beautiful piece of art, a Greek statue, a peasant by Millet, a Dutch portrait or a nude woman by Courbet or Degas moves him, 'the enjoyment of a beautiful thing is like coitus, a moment of infinity'. (B.12)

His looking at sexuality and painting as incompatible alternatives becomes comprehensible if we realize that in fact unconsciously, and for his own particular reasons, he has equated sexuality and painting: for him they are one and the same thing. Thus if he paints as he does, in a frenzy, his sexual desire is exhausted and he becomes more or less impotent. Similarly, his perception that a more frequent and freer sexual life than the very methodic, at best once a fortnight sexual outlet that he allows himself, will drain him of his creativity and ability to paint, is quite correct. The energy for his painting is modified sexual energy and if he expends it on the one activity it will not be available for the other. He says of Milliet [the Zouave officer who was his friend] 'Milliet is lucky, he has as many Arlesiennes as he wants; but then he cannot paint them, and if he were a painter he would not get them.' (542) The parallel between sexuality and painting finds further confirmation in statements such as the following, 'I also feel the possibility of going to seed and of seeing the day of one's capacity for artistic creation pass, just as a man loses his virility in the course of his life.

'That is inevitable, and naturally in this as in the other, the one thing to do is to be of good heart and strike while the iron is hot'. (530)

The parallel becomes even clearer: 'I can very well do without God both in my life and in my painting, but I cannot, ill as I am do without something which is greater that I, which is my life – the power to create. And if, frustrated in the physical power, a man tries to create thoughts instead of children, he is still part of humanity.' (531) (In the context of the letter 'thoughts' in this passage are used as the equivalent of paintings). And similarly when he writes: 'If a painter ruins his character by working hard at painting, a thing which leaves him useless for many other things, for family life etc., etc.' (514)

Freud has described how for certain people 'The thought-process itself becomes sexualized, for the sexual pleasure which is normally attached to the content of thought becomes shifted on to the act of thinking itself, and the satisfaction derived from reaching the conclusion of a line of thought is experienced as a *sexual* satisfaction'.[1]

All the above leads to the following hypothesis in relation to the type of sublimation that is to be observed in operation not only in Vincent, but in some other artists, in all branches of art. There is no question that the sexual energy used by Vincent in his work was sufficiently modified in some specific ways as not to interfere with the artist's ability to create or with the performance of such ego functions as are required in the process of painting. It is a well-established clinical finding of psychoanalysis that excessive sexualization of certain activities of the personality, of its ego functions, frequently leads to an incapacity in the performance of the functions or activities involved, that is to a neurotic inhibition of such functions. Nevertheless in Vincent's case some of the sexual qualities were sufficiently unmodified as to make the pursuit of the activity pleasurable, the performance of the particular ability a most gratifying experience with many of the characteristics of orgasm. Vincent's frenzy to paint that become his only sustenance and purpose in life, and the incredible number of paintings he was able to produce in such a short space of time as seven years (around nine hundred oil paintings) become thus more understandable. I believe that similar phenomena can be discerned in scientists and artists in all fields.

Perhaps the explanation lies in the fact that what is sexualized is the final product, the work of art as such, while the functions involved in its production use sufficiently neutralized energy as not to be interfered with in any important way.

Many artists, and certainly Van Gogh, have a very special relationship to their creations, perhaps particularly so while they are being created. The study of such relationships could prove very enlightening. In Vincent's case it is evident that the production of paintings is equated with procreation and the conception of children; it is in fact a sublimation of these wishes. Many times, as we have shown, he refers to producing pictures as 'giving birth' to a picture. In his case the phantasy extends further to include his brother as an essential partner in the creation of these 'babies'. He is in his unconscious phantasies fecundated by Theo, on the basis of his passive-feminine phantasies. He says, 'I swear that you will have created them [the paintings – babies] as much as I,

[1] Freud, S., 'A Case of Obsessional Neurosis', *S.E.*, Vol. 10, p. 245.

and that we are making them together'. (538) In this way painting was a most useful sublimatory outlet for his passive-feminine phantasies. I do not claim that what I have described applies generally to all artistic productions or artists. I only claim that this seems to me to describe with reasonable accuracy some of the mechanisms involved in Van Gogh's artistic production and perhaps in a number of other very outstanding and original artists'.

Eissler in his book, *Leonardo da Vinci, Psychoanalytic Notes on the Enigma,* points to how in the case of the genius one may have to consider the psychopathology in a different light and take into account the possibly indispensable role that it plays in special achievements. This is certainly a necessity in the case of Vincent Van Gogh. Eissler says: 'If we wish to apply seriously to the study of the psychology of genius the principle of psychic determinism, we may have to take his psychopathology into account as one of the factors indispensable to his genius-hood. Consequently if what we observed in the genius struck us as neurotic or psychotic or perverse or even criminal, we would then have to reconsider our classification under these accustomed headings. If for example, an apparently obssesional symptom were observed and it turned out that that sympton was indispensable to geniushood in that case, there would be no sense in calling it a neurotic symptom. Whatever the essence of a neurosis may be, the concept of neurosis makes sense only when it is correlated with a deficit. No doubt, neurotic symptoms may facilitate socially approved behaviour, or, at least, a person may by means of disease have gained the advantages we actually observe him to be in possession of. Yet, there is no known achievement which would justify the claim that is necessitated by observations in the instance of the genius, mainly, that there was no alternative path, for him, to that achievement.'

I should complete this chapter by calling attention to the fact that though there are a number of great paintings of Van Gogh's belonging to any one of the previous periods, it was really in the Arles period and from then on that most of his greatest paintings were produced. Up to then Vincent had kept a hope of finding a woman to marry and of raising a family. He had not given himself up completely to painting, there were other longings and other phantasies. Even during the Paris period he had frequently in mind the idea of getting married, and more than once suggested to Theo that the sooner both of them got married the better. He was particularly insistent on this argument when he decided to join Theo in Paris, in this case partly at least as a protection against too close a relationship between himself and his brother – that is, as a defence against his passive-feminine longings. Somewhat later, as we have seen, he was prepared to marry Theo's mistress. And in the periods that preceded the Paris one there were several incidents with which we are already familiar: the Ursula episode in London, his falling in love with his cousin Kee at Etten, his living together with Sien, the prostitute, whom he wanted to marry during The Hague period, his short-lived affair with Margot Begemann during the Nuenen period, and a number of adventures during the Paris period the nature of which is not well known to us due to the absence of correspondence with his brother during this time.

When he moved to the south, to Arles, he renounced all his ambitions in the direction of women, marriage and a family. Furthermore his potency was weak and his sexual life became very restricted. It was then that painting took, almost completely, the place of his sexuality, and became in fact his sexual life, his only source of gratification, his only aim and purpose in life. Now all this energy was channelled into his painting, so that in about two years he produced a prodigious number of paintings: about 415 out of the total of 840 oil paintings he produced throughout his complete artistic life. We should remember that Vincent turned to painting only during the last ten years of his life. between twenty-seven to thirty-seven, and that during the first three years of this period he devoted himself more or less completely to drawing and an occasional water colour. Thus his oil painting period is reduced to seven years of which the last two and a half which we are now considering, though the more disturbed of his life, were as productive in quantity as the other five years put together. This gives clearly the measure of the role that his sexual conflicts contributed not only to his output as a painter but to the quality of his work.

❧ 18 ❧

FEAR OF SUCCESS
AND FEAR OF FAILURE

ONE finds in Vincent Van Gogh a curious mixture: an intense fear of being successful combined with a no less intense fear of failure – and side by side with the fear of success an intense longing to be successful. There is every indication of intense conflicts in these different directions, the nature of which deserves further examination. This peculiar admixture can be noted all through his life, but it became more marked during the Amsterdam period when he was preparing for the university entrance examinations. We have seen how he struggled and how he hoped that God would allow him to be successful. He considered it a struggle for his life, nothing less and nothing more. In the end, as we know, he abandoned his studies, failing once again as he had failed previously as an art dealer – to the great disappointment of his family, especially of his father and his rich uncle Vincent, in whose steps in a successful career as an art-dealer he was meant to follow. One cannot escape the impression that there were specific factors, specific phantasies and unconscious conflicts, which forced him from one failure to another – quite independently of the serious emotional disturbance that overcame him in London, which was in itself an important contributing factor to his inability to reach whatever aims he set himself, to make use of his great potential and undoubted intellectual capacities or to relate to others.

We have discussed the multiplicity of reasons that determined his failure as an evangelist preacher during the Borinage period.

When he became a painter the situation was very similar. At first he was extremely reluctant to take certain progressive steps such as the move from drawing into water colour and oil painting.

He feared, on a conscious level, that such attempts would prove a failure, that he might not have the necessary gifts and capacities for it and this thought paralysed him. Again and again he rationalized his reluctance to take the step with all sorts of intellectual arguments. It was only under the influence and gentle but firm pressure of his brother Theo, on whose goodwill he was totally dependent, that he took the step into colour and into the media of oils.

It is quite possible that without Theo's support, influence and guiding light when there were crucial steps to be taken, Vincent would never have developed as an artist and a painter to the position he was finally able to reach. During the whole of Vincent's career Theo had the unique ability to make him take what were essential steps in his development, then he would move quickly to the background again in order to allow Vincent complete and absolute freedom to develop in his work. Another interesting example in this respect is Vincent's change of palette from the dark subdued tones he started with to those of the brilliant colourist he was to become. Vincent again was most reluctant to change his own palette for some time. Theo's gentle influence at first in his letters, and later on in Paris, introducing Vincent to the work of the impressionists that he admired and championed as an art dealer, brought about the change that led Aurier to describe Vincent's paintings as 'symphonies in colour'. Without his brother's help and the special relationship that existed between them it is doubtful that Vincent would have developed as he was in fact able to do. He certainly had all the potentialities but too many conflicts interfered and these potentialities required special conditions to fulfil themselves, such as a great deal of encouragement and unconditional artistic, moral and economic support, as well as a protected environment for Vincent himself. All this and more Theo provided generously. Vincent was fully aware of this and frequently stated that whatever he achieved in the future they would have achieved together.

From the very beginning Vincent was reluctant to show or to attempt to sell his work. There were occasional exceptions to this rule at which times he would as we have seen, bitterly accuse his patient brother Theo of not wanting to exhibit his work, of not trying to sell it. The drive that overcame his usual reluctance and hesitation at such times was his love for a woman and his strong

ent painted several versions of the sower. Unmarried and childless as he
he always admired the ability of the peasant to fecundate Mother Earth,
as he admired Gauguin for having children. The painting is highly symbolic
the trees as a powerful phallic symbol, the seed and Mother Earth being
regnated and at the back of it all the warmth of the fiery sun. (See Chapter
Vincent's Conflicts Around Sexuality, Their Influence on his Paintings,
143.)

o by courtesy of the Amsterdam Municipal Museum

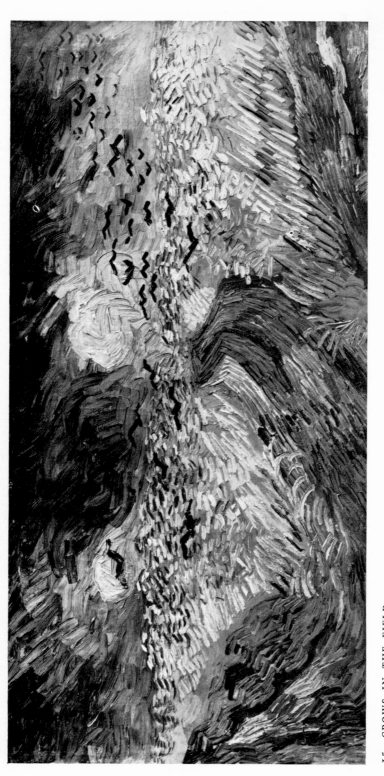

15. CROWS IN THE FIELD

This impressive picture was the last Van Gogh ever painted. The sky is closing down on the painter, while the crows fly towards him. It is perhaps the only one of his paintings where some lack of control is to be noticed. There are two suns in the sky and the perspective is disrupted by roads that depart in several directions. Nevertheless the dramatic impact and beauty of the painting remains unimpaired. (See Chapter 15, Vincent's Mental Illness, page 124.)

desire to become financially independent in order to marry her. We are familiar with such episodes from previous descriptions of his love for his cousin Kee, and later on for Sien. It is an interesting speculation to imagine how much the course of events would have changed had it been possible for him to fulfil such wishes. Without such motivation his usual fears controlled the ground again and his interest in such matters was reduced.

Already during The Hague period, sometime around September or October 1882, when he wrote to Rappard trying to console him for the rejection of some work he had sent for an exhibition at 'Arti', he stated that he had never had a similar experience himself 'for the simple reason that I don't even dream of exhibiting my work. The idea leaves me absolutely cold. Now and then I wish some friends could have a look at what I have in my studio – which happens very seldom; but I have never felt the wish and I think I never shall – to invite the general public to look at my work. I am not indifferent to appreciation of my work, but this too must be something silent – and I think a certain popularity the least desirable thing of all'. (R.16)

By the time he was at Arles these conflicts had acquired their fullest intensity and were expressed in some of his letters. Not infrequently in the same letter there are references to the two sides of these conflicts. Thus he says, 'It is a gloomy enough prospect to have to say to myself that perhaps the painting I am doing will never be of any value whatever . . . anyhow I must go on and try to do better'. (524) Later on in the same letter he quotes the words of one of Zola's characters in *L'Oeuvre*, 'You think, you poor souls, that when an artist has established his talent and his reputation, he is safe. On the contrary, henceforth he is denied producing anything which is not perfect. His reputation itself forces him to take more pains over his work, as the chances of selling grow fewer. At the least sign of weakness, the whole jealous pack will fall on him and destroy that very reputation and the faith that the changeable and treacherous public has temporarily had in him'. (524) He quotes Carlyle, 'You know the glow-worms in Brazil that shine so that in the evening ladies stick them into their hair with pins, well, fame is a fine thing, but look you, to the artist it is what the hairpin is to the insects'. Then he adds, 'So I have a horror of success, I am afraid of "the morning after the night before" of an impressionist success, even these difficult days will later seem to us "the good good old times!" ' (524), and 'I neither care about success for myself nor about happiness'. (524) He wrote in the same way about Gauguin who was hoping for success and 'doesn't realize the eternity of poverty . . . but for our own part let's keep our utter indifference to success or failure'. (524)

A few weeks later he would write, 'Fortunately for me, I do not hanker after victory any more, and all that I seek in painting is a way to make life bearable'. (529)

With respect to selling he showed a similar ambivalence, 'As to selling I say you are certainly right not to go out of your way looking for sales, I certainly should prefer never to sell, if it could be'. (555) This type of extreme statement was frequently a reaction to the disappointment of not selling which implied that his paintings were not acceptable to the public. Any criticism of his work had frequently, as we have observed, a devastating effect on him and led to the wish to withdraw altogether from being exposed to it.

Though we have come across innumerable examples of his reactions to criticism in general and to criticisms of his work in particular perhaps one of the best illustrations of this can be found in his correspondence with his friend the painter van Rappard. Vincent had sent him a lithograph of 'The Potato Eaters' and the former had written critically about it. Vincent returned the letter; he felt insulted and demanded an apology that was not forthcoming. In spite of receiving no answer he wrote several letters where one finds a combination of atrocious abuse and an intense and tender wish for reconciliation with his friend. He wrote that he had never been very useful as a friend, 'for amice, you were distressingly little useful to me – and don't think it ill of me if for the first and last time I tell you flatly – I don't know a drier friendship than yours'. (R.52) He denied that he was hurt by Rappard's comments, but reading these letters one can see how deeply hurt he was. He said that Rappard had behaved like many others including his parents, teachers, and Messrs Goupil and Co, but he was not obliged 'to listen to their everlasting drivel'. (R.53) He claimed he did not care at all about these things while at the same time he kept demanding an apology, 'I want you to take back, frankly and without reservation, what you wrote in your last letters'. (R.53) At the same time he wrote that their dispute had a ridiculous side to it and that they ought to be sensible and put a stop to the argument. Rappard remained silent and Vincent's irritation increased further, 'To my regret I have not yet discovered any reply from you. The more I think about it the more I feel that I shall personally not be at all sorry to be done with you – unless you withdraw once and for all a correspondence that – in my opinion – is hardly a credit to you . . . I am willing to look upon the whole business as a misunderstanding . . . In case you do not write this week – *I no longer desire your reply*. And then time will tell whether your remarks about my work and my person were justified or not.' (R.56) Rappard finally responded to this last appeal but the relationship between the friends had suffered a blow from which it was not to recover. The correspondence ceased soon afterwards, Rappard regretting this in a letter to Vincent's mother after his death.

Vincent knew on the other hand that his attitude to selling was completely unrealistic and at times hoped that he could sell if only to repay Theo his expenses. When Gauguin was at Arles with him and sold several pictures he wrote, 'I believe that the time will come when I too shall sell, but I am so far behind with you, and while I go on spending, I bring nothing in. Sometimes the thought of it saddens me'. (557)

Nevertheless, he used all sorts of excuses to postpone exhibiting whenever there was an opportunity. Towards the end of October 1888 he wrote to his brother, 'Let's quietly postpone exhibiting until I have some 30 canvases. Then we are going to exhibit them only once in your appartment for our friends, and even then without exercising any pressure. And don't let's do anything else'. (558)

Sometime during November 1889 he received a letter inviting him to exhibit at the *Révue Indépendante* as he had previously agreed to do. Now, using as an excuse the fact that they were asking for a picture as an exhibitor's fee he wrote that he had changed his mind 'so no exhibition at the Révue Indépendante'. (561) In the same letter he wrote to Theo, 'We have hardly exhibited, have we? There have been a few canvases, first at Tanguy's, afterwards at Thomas's, and then at Martin's.

'Now as for myself, I tell you flatly that I can see no use even in that, and it really seems to me much better if you simply keep the studies you like in your apartment and send the others back here rolled up, since the apartment is small, and if you kept everything, they would crowd it up.

'Then, without hurrying ourselves, I am going on down here, getting the stuff ready for a more serious exhibition . . . Now as to showing a few canvases at Tanguy's and Thomas's it's a matter of such indifference to me that it isn't worth talking about, but above all remember that I simply don't care. I already know what I shall do the moment I have enough canvases. Right now I am only concerned with making them.' (561)

When Theo proposed that Vincent have a small canvas exhibited at Goupil, Vincent refused again, 'If it is either to please me, as for my own advantage, then on the contrary I'm of the opinion that it is absolutely unnecessary. If you asked me what would please me it's just this one thing; that you keep in the apartment for yourself whatever you like out of my work, and sell none of it now'. (563) He was at this point rather upset by some friend's criticisms of his work as not well finished, done in too much of a hurry. He reacted with the usual withdrawal, writing to Theo, 'You will lose nothing by waiting a little for my work, and we will calmly leave our comrades to despise the present ones. Fortunately for me, I know well enough what I want, and am basically indifferent to the criticism that I work too hurriedly. In answer to that, I have done some things even more hurriedly these last few days'. (563)

After the first mental breakdown at Arles he wrote again, 'Only I think that we must still keep quiet with regard to my own painting. If you want any pictures, certainly I can send you some already, but when my peace of mind comes back to me, I hope to do different things. However as to the Independants, do what seems best to you, and what the others do'. (568)

In September 1889 he was invited to participate in the next exhibition of the Vingtistes. He was on the whole pleased, but even then there is some hesitation and ambivalence. 'I should very much like to exhibit there, though I feel my inferiority beside so many of the Belgians, who have tremendous talent.' Later on in the same letter he explained to Theo that he was doing two pictures, 'The Reaper' and a 'Self-Portrait' that were just right 'for the Vingtistes, if indeed they remember me at the right moment, but then I am absolutely indifferent to it all, perhaps it is even preferable if they should forget me'. (604) In the end he exhibited two other pictures.

When Isaäcson, a painter and art critic, wanted to write an

article about his work he felt very distressed and wrote to him, 'As it is possible that in your next article you will put in a few words about me, I will repeat my scruples, so that you will not go beyond a *few* words, because it is *absolutely certain* that I shall never do important things'. (614a) He told his mother too that Isaäcson intended writing about his work in a Dutch newspaper but he had asked him not to do so. To his sister W. he wrote in even more expressive terms, 'Isaäcson wants to write an article about me in one of the Dutch papers, on the subject of pictures which are exactly like those I am sending you, but reading such an article would make me very sad, and I wrote to tell him so'. (W.15)

Towards the end of 1889 he had another crisis and when Dr Peyron asked if he wanted finally to exhibit at the Vingtistes, in his confusion he refused again. Fortunately, once recovered he changed his mind, mainly for Theo's sake, and pictures were sent to the exhibition.

During January 1890 an article by Albert Aurier appeared in the *Mercure de France*. Theo sent the article to him enclosed with a letter where he informed Vincent that he was the father of a little boy. Vincent was immensely flattered by the article on the one hand but on the other he felt very disturbed by it. His diverse reactions to this article are very illuminating. He thought that Theo should send the article to Gauguin, and explained that these things ought to be said of Gauguin and not of him. Perhaps he suggested to Theo, they ought to be sent too to Reid and Tersteeg, the latter his old boss at The Hague when he worked for Goupil. As we remember the painter had innumerable difficulties with him, many of them springing from Vincent's idea that Tersteeg did not think anything of him as an artist. It is in some ways rèmarkable that now that he had reached some substantial success, he did not take advantage of it to show them how much in the wrong they had been. Not only had this article been written, loudly acclaiming him as a painter, but his paintings were attracting a great deal of attention, especially among some important and well-known contemporary artists.

At last he had made a sale in an exhibition; one of his paintings at the Brussel's exhibition had been sold for 400 francs! But there was a great deal more to go with all this. Theo had been sending him much good news about his work.

At the 'Independents' he exhibited two pictures, the 'Irises' and 'The Starlit Night'. Though he did not sell them the 'Irises' especially was admired by many people who talked to Theo about it. The 'XX' (Vingtistes) wanted his paintings too. Lauzet, the lithographer of Vincent's much admired Monticelli, was appreciative of his works and was to make lithographs of some. Lauzet too greatly admired his drawings.

At the exhibition of the XX at Brussels, his paintings were successful; Theo wrote, 'I read in a paper that the canvases which arouse the curiosity of the public the most are the open-air study of Cezanne, the landscapes by Sisley, the symphonies by Van Gogh and the works of Renoir'. (T.25) Theo concluded in his letter that now they could wait for success to come, 'you will surely live to see it'. (T.25) Mans, the organizer of the exhibition, thanked him for his participation in the salon of the XX, 'where he has found many lively artistic sympathies in the confusion of the discussion'. (T.29) Gauguin said that Vincent's pictures at the XX 'were the chief attraction at the exhibition, the *clou*' (T.29) Pisarro stated that Vincent had achieved real success at this exhibition. Diaz stopped Theo in the street asking him to send Vincent his compliments, 'Tell him that his pictures are highly remarkable'. (T.32) Monet said that Vincent's pictures were the best of all in the exhibition. Serret was enraptured. And so on, and so on.

To all these triumphs Vincent showed very little positive reaction. In fact, as we know, they were to make a significant contribution to his many mental breakdowns from the end of February 1889. From this we can deduce the intensity of the conflicts aroused by his success.

On the other hand he was in a way frightened and complained that Aurier's article placed too much responsibility on him; 'It must be understood that my back is not broad enough to carry such an undertaking'. (625)

To Aurier he wrote a letter of thanks. He praised the article 'as a work of art in itself' but considered that the comments about himself were greatly exaggerated, saying that 'he felt uneasy that what you say is due to others rather than to myself'. (626a) Most of the credit given to him he said ought to go in reality to Monticelli and to Gauguin, to both of whom he owed much and to some others. *'For the part that is allotted to me, or will*

be allotted to me, will remain, I assure you, very secondary'. (626a)
Nevertheless, as a token of his gratitude Vincent sent Aurier one
of his new studies on Cypresses.

To his mother too he wrote talking of his success and of the sale
of one of his paintings, but he could allow himself the enjoyment
of this victory to a limited degree only. There were powerful
unconscious reasons that seriously interfered with his moment of
triumph. To the mother he qualified his success, though admitting
that at times he was cheered by it. 'I was rather surprised at the
article they wrote about me. Isaäcson wanted to do one some time
ago, and I asked him not to; I was sorry when I read it, because
it is so exaggerated; the problem is different – what sustains me
in my work is the very feeling that there are several others doing
the same thing I am, so why an article on me and not on those
six or seven others, etc?' (627) Significantly there were six Van
Gogh's siblings who lived and seven including his dead elder
brother. Thus this innocent remark may well be an expression of
guilt because of his earlier sibling rivalry. Why should he who
complained of not being treated like his siblings, be favoured by
fate in this way? His distress increased and he ended by having
another crises, this time a short one lasting only one week. Then
he wrote again to his mother and sister, 'As soon as I heard that my
work was having some success, and read the article in question, I
feared at once that I should be punished for it; this is how things
nearly always go in a painter's life: success is about the worst
thing that can happen'. (629a) In real despair he wrote to Theo,
'Please ask Mr Aurier not to write any more articles about my
painting, insist upon this, that to begin with he is mistaken about
me, since I am too overwhelmed with grief to face publicity'. (629)
Nevertheless two months later when he felt better he wrote to the
Ginoux (at Arles) telling them about the articles in the paper and
the success of his paintings with the public.

His massive fears of success, his conviction that he would be
punished severely for having achieved some success, point to an
insurmountable situation of conflict and of guilt, the sources of
which I will attempt to trace.

We have earlier described while discussing his relationship to
Sien how one of the most important among many reasons for his
fear was related to his curious need to provoke punishment and
rejection. Psychoanalysis has long since discovered that such a

need for punishment is usually the result of great unconscious guilt for 'crimes' which individuals believe they have committed and of which they have not the slightest conscious awareness. In reality their behaviour frequently is, or always has been, more or less irreproachable; consequently they have no conscious feelings which they can identify with the inner experience of feeling guilty. The only thing that betrays the existence of the guilt is their constant provocation of punishment and rejection by others in their everyday behaviour. Vincent belonged to this group of people. I have already mentioned how much of this guilt is related to sexuality and presumably to masturbatory activity which he believed had ruined him both physically and mentally.

There can be little doubt for the analytically minded that much of his difficulty in exhibiting his work was based on the existence of important exhibitionistic conflicts. Exhibitionism generally involves primarily the wish to expose the genital organs to another person. Such wishes can be very conflictive, and frequently find outlets in alternative displaced and socially acceptable forms of exhibitionism, such as dressing in striking clothes, exhibiting the results of one's activities and so on. For the latter purpose painting as a profession is a particularly suitable vehicle. Vincent was of course able to achieve a limited degree of gratification in this sublimated way though on the whole even the exhibition of his paintings remained a highly conflictive area. Perhaps one of the best examples of Vincent's strong exhibitionistic tendencies is to be found in a letter to his sister W. where he wrote, that when Gauguin arrived, they would go to Marseilles, 'It is my firm intention to saunter in the Cannebiere, there dressed exactly like Monticelli, as I have seen his portrait, with an enormous yellow hat, a black velvet jacket, white trousers, yellow gloves, a bamboo cane, and with a grand southern air'. (W.8)

If phallic exhibitionism and its derivatives can be conflictive the other possible forms of exhibitionism are not less so. Vincent's dirty appearance and clothes were at least in part determined by strong anal exhibitionistic tendencies; he displayed the worst, dirtiest parts of himself. His paintings were in this respect, not only his babies but his faeces – this partly explains his reluctance to sell them, to exhibit them, to part with them, and his at times insurmountable fear of the criticism that their exposure might arouse in others.

Exhibitionistic tendencies furthermore are usually paired with similar strong scopophilic tendencies. I have mentioned earlier (Amsterdam period) how Vincent would attend public dances with the sole purpose of 'watching' people have fun. Similarly he was compelled to go and observe people who were mourning and see their reaction to death. On the whole Vincent's scopophilic tendencies seem to have found a most satisfactory outlet through painting, through looking at his own pictures and those of others, and through the further exercise of his childhood interests, such as the observation of nature in order to find subjects for his paintings.

Another set of factors belongs in the relationship to his father and his oedipal rivalry with him. The Reverend Van Gogh had not been a very successful man in real life, especially in contrast to several of his brothers who had been quite successful in their respective fields of action. He achieved little in his clerical career, remaining always a peasant's pastor in charge of very small congregations. He too had a very special relationship with his brother Vincent, the successful art dealer (Vincent and Theo again). This is in itself an interesing parallel with the painter's dependence, economic and otherwise, on his brother Theo.

Vincent was very aware of his father's position and at least on one occasion that we have referred to earlier, he became very angry when his employer Mr Braat pointed out that there was little future in the career in the church on which he had set his heart, after all he had only to consider his father's situation to see this clearly. Vincent protested: he had at that time an idealized picture of his father who, as far as he was concerned, was in the right place, where a good Christian ought to be, as a modest pastor with a brethren of peasants. He had made a strong identification with this image of his father and did not want to be any better than him, in fact he could not be any better than him. When this idealization broke down and Vincent started to despise the father and his profession he remained more than ever unconsciously tied by this identification. To be successful as a painter acquired the meaning of an aggressive act against his father especially after the innumerable quarrels between them. He felt that he must never do better or be more successful than his oedipal rival. On the other hand there was the fact that the Reverend did think that nothing very much would come of Vincent generally, or of his work as a painter in particular. And Vincent's work had to comply with these predictions, in part out of a childhood fear of the powerful father. His success would be like a terrible blow to his father who would thus be proved wrong for everybody to see. For such reasons he felt compelled to write to Aurier that he did not deserve to be praised in the way Aurier had done; such praise ought to go to Gauguin who, as we have seen, was a father substitute figure in his unconscious. All praise ought to go to the all powerful father whose powers of retaliation he still feared unconsciously. For this reason he still feared success associating it with terrible punishments that would befall him. For similar unconscious reasons he did not want his nephew to be called after him but after his own father and his brother Theo. To do anything else was to rob the father of his rights – by now, after his mental breakdowns, he was again thinking a great deal about his father and regretted much of his behaviour towards him.

Though all the above could easily be a sufficient explanation for his fear of success it does not sufficiently explain the concomitant fear of failure and of criticisms. I have already many times referred to an element in Vincent's history which played an essential role in his development and in the distortion of his personality. Indeed it looms heavily everywhere and is an essential part to the background of Vincent's character. I refer to the impact on his family, and through them on him, of the stillbirth of his older brother for whom he was meant to substitute and whose name he was given. We have mentioned some psycho-analytic studies of families where a child has been conceived to take the place of a dead one.[1] In Vincent's case the brother, being stillborn, had never had an identity of his own in reality, but for this very reason an ideal one had been created in the phantasy life of the parents. He would have been the perfect child, the compendium of all virtue, ability and kindness. He would always have done everything right, and, especially where Vincent failed, the other, the dead Vincent, would have been successful. This extreme degree of idealization of a dead child is by no means uncommon and such were the ideals of behaviour and accomplishment which his parents offered unconsciously to Vincent for emulation. This explains the high ego-ideals which he set himself, his dread of failing (exhibiting his painting always implied the risk of failing), and his fear of success (quite apart from the factors

[1] See page 14.

mentioned already), because there was always the risk that success would be transitory, in which case the later feelings of failure would become all the more painful. We have seen that he always dreaded this possibility. On the other hand, once successful, one is forced to perform at that very high standard all the time, or face great losses in terms of one's self-esteem. It is on a similar basis that we can understand his constant search for an identity, but always one of 'heroic proportions' such as that of a great Christian, a great painter, etc.

Against such high ego-ideals he would, of course, nearly always fall short. His badly battered ego needed to be shown some appreciation and admiration but the constant fear of not being up to these high standards forced him to withdraw from people and activities precisely out of the fear of criticisms that he felt certain he was to receive.

A further important aspect of these conflicts was the unconscious dread of competing with the *idealized dead Vincent*. Unconsciously he must have felt that his success was an attack on the memory of the dead one, an attempt to take his place in the affection of the parents. Such phantasies are highly conflictive since, as Cain points out, siblings of a dead child feel in some form responsible for their death even 'in the face of their not having even been born during the child's lifetime'. Cain further found that even in the phantasies of the parents, the substitute child was frequently felt to be responsible for the death of the dead one and that they could never accept the substitute sibling as being as good as the idealized dead one; in fact they tended to become increasingly disappointed from the moment of the birth onwards.

Furthermore, it seems possible that under these circumstances Vincent came to associate death and success. To be recognized as good as the brother or better even it was necessary to be dead like him, an association that may have made no small contribution to his fear of exhibiting and meeting success and would justify and explain his feeling of impending disaster and punishment as expressed to his sister after Aurier's article, his successful exhibitions and so on. It is indeed not surprising that under the impact of such unconscious pressures his mind collapsed.

Painting was in a way a most suitable area of activity for this type of conflict since as Vincent well knew and frequently stated, it is a profession where one can be considered an utter failure during one's lifetime only to rise to fame after death; a possibility well adapted to his unconscious requirements. In this sense his recognition as an outstanding painter came perhaps too soon.

❧ 19 ☙

FURTHER COMMENTS ON HIS
RELATIONSHIP TO THEO
AND TO OTHERS

In previous chapters we have become familiar with the nature of Vincent's relationship to his brother Theo and to others. We have seen innumerable examples of his many difficulties in this area and of his sensitivity and reactions to criticism and rejection by friends and relatives, as well as his response to disappointments in the sphere of love. To complete the impressions thus gained it remains only to highlight a number of specific aspects.

What, for instance were the reasons that led to the unique relationship between Vincent and Theo? In retrospect we can only conclude that Vincent grew up with a feeling of not having been sufficiently loved by his parents.

Much of his hostility and aggressive behaviour towards them in later years was a reaction to this feeling, openly expressed in his letters to Theo and in his arguments with the parents. He made many attempts to force them to acknowledge the damage he felt he had suffered because of this and to redress the situation. This we saw most clearly during the Nuenen period (1883–5) when he was embittered by their lack of repentance about having banished him from home two years earlier. Obviously these complaints about events of later years were the unconscious vehicle for feelings and complaints that belonged in the early years of his life, and at a later stage, his having been sent to boarding school, to The Hague and to London. He always hoped for a reconciliation but it had to be a reconciliation on his own terms and these were unacceptable to the parents. Being unsuccessful with them he frequently tried to recreate a parent-child relationship in his relationship to others, attempts that of necessity always had to end in failure.

Nobody could possibly have played such a role with Vincent, no longer a small child but a grown man and a difficult one at that. But there was one exception, his brother Theo. For many years Vincent avoided a direct confrontation with these feelings and the accompanying phantasies by different means including, in particular the idealization of his family, especially of his parents. If they were perfect, as he made them in his phantasy, there was no ground for any complaints or doubts about their feelings for *all* their children, including himself. We have had the opportunity to see how at a given point this carefully developed defensive attitude started to collapse and his enormous resentment and his complaints of being unloved and unwanted, in fact, of being treated like the family dog, broke through in all violence.

I should make clear that there is sufficient evidence to affirm that Vincent's complaints were not by any means totally unfounded. Some of the reasons that determined a distorted relationship between Vincent and his parents were existent even before he was conceived, having been triggered off by fate through the death of his namesake. Nor is there any question that Vincent's complaints were very much magnified by his own personal perception and interpretation of the parental attitudes (as is the rule in such cases). There was undoubtedly much of a positive nature in the parents' relationship to him. Nevertheless for the first two years of his life Vincent grew in the shadow of his dead brother and it is clear that later on some of his siblings, especially Theo, were openly preferred to him – a situation that Vincent's abnormal and difficult behaviour may have done much to create.

We have observed some manifestations of the impact of his brother's death on his personality for example his curious behaviour and reactions when confronted with death, particularly the death of children, for instance the two children drowned in a canal in Amsterdam. Even more noticeable, was his nearly morbid interest in the feelings and mourning of the relatives, especially the parents.

Similarly we have seen his marked concern for the safety of Sien and her baby at the time of her delivery, and later for the safety of Jo and her baby. In his letters from Ramsgate to his brother – at a time when he was obsessed by religious ideas – he occasionally quoted passages from his religious readings which clearly showed this type of concern.

'Can a woman forget her sucking child, that she should not have compassion on the son of her womb? . . .

'A voice was heard in Ramah, lamentation and bitter weeping, Rachel weeping for her children refused to be comforted for her children, because they were not.' (82a) Or his own comment, 'How often the memory of one already gone to my Father's house – where there are many mansions – has warmed me and made my heart glow with love on my evening walks through the streets of London'. (82a)

When he was two years old sister Anna was born, an event that could not but bring forward his hostility to the new rival. It is not surprising that this sister recalled him in later years as always teasing her. When by the next year, Theo, his third sibling was born, a close relationship developed between them from the start. This is not surprising: the first child in the family often joins forces with the third against the second, more resented, rival. Furthermore, since much of his sibling rivalry found outlets and was perhaps exhausted in the relationship to his sister Anna, he could come close to Theo, trying in the relationship to him to make up for what he felt missing in the relationship to the parents. I believe that in this way the foundation of the relationship between the brothers was laid down. Much was to be added to it in later years. It is very possible that deep in Vincent's unconscious some connection between the dead brother and Theo was established, a connection perhaps reinforced by the fact that much of the parental love moved from the dead brother to Theo, by-passing Vincent. Theo became in due time an obvious favourite with the parents, not of course without many good reality reasons. This was a painful fact that Vincent came to recognize and verbalize at different points in his life. It was out of such awareness that in later life he asked Theo on repeated occasions to use his privileged position with the parents to influence them in his favour. It is possible that some of Vincent's demands on his brother were based on the phantasy, 'give to me since you took away from me'. It is similarly possible that, because of the unconscious link between Theo and the dead brother, Vincent established very strong defences against the expression of hostility towards Theo to protect him from his death wishes – defences that proved successful much of the time though obviously not all the time.

When Theo, at the age of fifteen, was sent to Brussels as an apprentice art dealer as he himself had been four years earlier Vincent was overwhelmed with sympathy for his brother. He saw himself again in Theo as a young boy, sent away from home and full of anxiety. He reacted by writing many consoling and reassuring letters including much advice to Theo. Through this narcissistic identification with his brother's distress the tie to him became stronger. Vincent wanted to reassure and comfort him as he himself would have liked to be comforted when at the age of sixteen he was sent to The Hague.

Both brothers, young and inexperienced as they were, needed each other for the exchange of confidences about life and the world, confidences that were not for the 'pastor-father's ears'. Vincent's needs were far greater than Theo's in this respect, especially later, when he became withdrawn and hardly able to mix with and relate to his contemporaries. Theo played in this respect a most essential role throughout Vincent's life. He was to Vincent a more benign father figure, a more human and less severe super-ego than that represented by the highly moral and self-righteous parson-father with whom he had started to find it impossible to discuss anything or to show any human weaknesses without suffering a severe reprimand or a severe blow to his self-esteem, through imagined or actual criticisms and rejections. Theo was very kind natured and closer to Vincent in outlook. He was able to take a more liberal view than existed in the suffocating religious milieu at home, and they shared confidences and a common interest in art.

With his further withdrawal after the severe emotional breakdown in London Vincent was more in need of his brother than ever. Theo was one of the few, perhaps the only one, with whom he was able to communicate freely and to talk of his longings and anxieties about past shortcomings and the possible failure of his new efforts – such as for instance passing his examinations in Amsterdam.

We should note that when he went to the mining district of the Borinage where he was absorbed by his work and communicated more freely with other human beings on the basis of their many miseries and necessities, the need to correspond and communicate with Theo was greatly diminished. This fact deserves special attention, in his later life as a painter even when he was more

5. SUN-FLOWERS

incent's beloved Sunflowers, of which there are several versions were
inted by him as part of the decoration to Gauguin's room in the
llow House at Arles. 'The sunflowers are mine' he said once, and no
her painter has depicted them so beautiful ever since. (See Chapter 16,
he Two Empty Chairs, page 134.)

'oto by courtesy of The Trustees, The National Gallery, London

17. VIEW AT AUVERS

Vincent spent the last few weeks of his life at Auvers. There he was under Dr Gauchet's care. Unfortunately, Gauchet though friendly and himself a lover of the arts and a painter, was a Cardiologist and had little understanding of the turmoils of the mind.

It was in the fields around this small town that Vincent shot himself on July 27, 1890. Two days later he died, just after saying, 'I wish I could die now'. His wish was granted, his misery came to an end. Few of the friends at his funeral realized that his death was a step into immortal absorbed by his work, he never failed to write to his brother; on the contrary, in some cases the more he painted the more he wrote. That this was so supports the view that painting was not a good substitute for his need for human contact and that the paintings themselves were done to a great extent for Theo's sake, as another form of communication and emotional contact with his brother. Some further confirmation of this point of view can be found in his signing his paintings only with his Christian name, just as he signed the letters to his brother. For purposes of communication with his brother, 'Vincent' was of course sufficient. He rationalized this behaviour by saying that Van Gogh was an impossible surname for foreigners to pronounce. If his paintings were to find their way to England and France his name would 'certainly be murdered'. (435e)

Two further, although less important, determinants for his use of his Christian name only in signing his paintings can be discerned. One was a grandiose phantasy, which proved to be correct, that it was not necessary for him to sign the paintings, 'they will surely recognize my work later on, and write about me when I am dead and gone'. (435c) Obviously if no name at all was really necessary, his Christian name was more than enough. The second was a protest against what he once called the 'trickerish Van Goghs', and had aggressive connotations against his family and his father in that he refused to use the family surname. After all he did not feel treated like a member of the family, so he was not really a Van Gogh.

Theo played many other roles in Vincent's unconscious as I have already described, among them that of father No. 2, and Vincent accordingly expected Theo to support him financially for much of his life. Vincent's type of dependence on and demandingness to his brother was of a very primitive nature having a distinct oral quality. The nature of this clinging and the feeling of hopelessness that accompanied any thought of his brother's withdrawing his support confirms the primitive nature of this tie. On the conscious level we see of course frequent signs of Vincent's conflicts in this respect, at which points he revolted against it and devised face-saving formulas such as that Theo was not supporting but buying his work. This primitive form of dependence helps to explain his catastrophic reactions to the threat of Theo's marriage and to the birth of Theo's son;

unconsciously he must have felt frightened, hopeless and helpless, like a small child when parental support is to be withdrawn.

The relationship was permeated as we have said by negative, aggressive, anal sadistic elements. For most of the time these were very much kept to the background, their intensity relatively less than that observed in his relationships to anybody else. Nevertheless these elements could flare up suddenly and become all important especially in reaction to frustrations of his oral dependence on the brother. Theo had always to provide for him economically, preferably as much as he demanded, in every circumstance, no matter how irrational, and in spite of the opposition of all others. He must always agree with Vincent's views and plans, or at least accept them with a certain tolerance and sympathy. Much of this is easily identifiable with the expectations of a young child from his parents and, in particular, can be understood in terms of the mother-child relationship. If Theo failed to give us this unconditional support Vincent's aggression and anal sadistic tendencies were triggered off, and found expression occasionally in extreme ambivalent feelings towards Theo or in sheer abuse of the brother.

Vincent had similar expectations from all those he related to and naturally enough nobody but his brother Theo, with his infinite patience and concern for him, was prepared to comply with such requirements while remaining supportive and uncritical. Thus it was a near impossibility for anybody to keep a close relationship to him for any length of time. Only Theo was capable of providing for him what has been described as a 'sheltered' environment.[1]

Similarly, many phallic-oedipal elements are found forming an integral part of the relationship as far as Vincent's unconscious phantasy life was concerned. Most outstanding among them was perhaps Vincent's passive-feminine identification and his phantasies of paintings as the equivalent of babies conceived by him through the agency of his brother. One such identification can be discerned in an incident already described when Vincent proposed to take Theo's mistress off his hands by marrying her so as to avoid a catastrophic reaction on the part of the girl if Theo parted with her. He said then 'you must part company – but how? . . . by treating her harshly you would immediately drive her to

[1] Professor G. Kraus.

suicide or insanity, and the repercussions on you would be sad indeed and leave you a broken man'. (460) On this occasion Vincent was unconsciously talking about how he would react if Theo were to reject him abruptly. It is this unconscious identification that partly explains Vincent's otherwise absurd plan to marry her (we have referred earlier to other determinants of this episode). He treats her well, as he hopes to be treated himself. It will not escape the reader that when Theo symbolically 'parted company' with him through getting married. Vincent found himself driven to insanity and suicide as he expected Theo's mistress to be.

We have seen how Vincent's ability to relate to others, and the nature of his relationships, changed at different periods of his life. At The Hague he was a charming young man with whom everybody wanted to deal. After London and the Ursula love affair, Vincent was a changed man and, with the anal regression that ensued, large amounts of aggression were released and he was at hard pains to cope with this. For some time, his embracing religion as he did, helped him to contain this aggression for most of the time; when provoked he was able to control himself for God's sake. Once this sublimatory outlet was no longer available he had little hope of controlling himself, a fact aggravated by his great sensitivity to criticisms. He was not without self-awareness in this respect and knew that it was through his own fault that many took him for a disagreable character, 'I am often terribly melancholy, irritable, hungering and thirsting, as it were, for sympathy; and when I do not get it, I try to act indifferently, speak sharply, and often even pour oil on the fire'. (208) Such awareness did not make him any more able to control himself, on the contrary he was usually overwhelmed by his feelings and talked and acted on impulse, only to regret it later on. It was in the end the fight against this excessive aggression that led him first to mutilate his own ear and later to destroy himself.

Similarly, after the London episode he became quite unable to deal with people in authority. He had to rebel against anybody in a position above him, intellectually or financially. We saw him quarrel with the house of Goupil until he was finally dismissed, with the ecclesiastical authorities in the Borinage, with his father, with Rev. Stricker, with his uncle Vincent, his friend Bernard's father, his siblings, Mr Tersteeg, Mauve, Gauguin, and all his friends in Paris. He became difficult, obstinate, opinionated and very critical. Yet any criticism gravely affected his self-esteem. Thus he was forced to turn violently against those people in authority whose demands he did not feel capable of fulfilling to their satisfaction. To preserve a bare minimum of self-esteem and well-being he would have considered, if necessary, that the whole world was wrong and against him, but much of this aggressive, defiant and obstinate behaviour was due largely to a basic feeling of insecurity and was his only means of coping and defence.

On the other hand, to those who were uncritical and who did not threaten his self-esteem, to the under-dog, the miners, the poor, the peasants, to Sien, to Roulin, to all animals, he was extremely tolerant, friendly, kind; he was capable of any sacrifice on their behalf.

⚘ 20 ⚘

VINCENT'S SUICIDE

VINCENT'S interest in death accompanied him through life for reasons we are familiar with. His general attitude to death and to suicide deserves some further consideration since he did, in fact, kill himself.

Originally his belief about death was typical for a fervent Christian, death being the step into eternal life in Christ. Later on, when his religious obsession had passed, he would occasionally wonder about the meaning of death asking what he referred to as the 'eternal question': 'Is the whole of life visible to us, or isn't it rather that on this side of death we see only one hemisphere?' (506) He wrote of how painters 'dead and buried' speak to the next generation or to several succeeding generations through their work. 'Is that all, or is there more to come? Perhaps death is not the hardest thing in a painter's life.' (506) He continued: 'For my own part I declare I know nothing whatever about it, but looking at the stars always makes me dream, as simply as I dream over the black dots representing towns and villages on a map. Why, I ask myself, shouldn't the shining dots of the sky be as accessible as the black dots of the map of France? Just as we take the train to get to Tarascon or Rouen, we take death to reach a star. One thing undoubtedly true in this reasoning is that we *cannot* get to a star while we are *alive*, any more than we can take the train when we are dead.' (506) These thoughts were triggered off by phantasies concerning Theo's death. The latter was ill and it was after asking how he was and what his doctor Gruby had said that Vincent embarked on these disquisitions.

At the time of his uncle Vincent's death he again wondered 'if life has yet another hemisphere, invisible it is true, but where one lands when one dies. To those who make this interesting and solemn journey, our best wishes and sympathy'. (516)

Though suicidal phantasies seem to have occurred quite early on in his life his early conscious attitude to it was that he was a man without such inclinations. Nevertheless, soon after this statement he felt deeply melancholic and may have become more aware of such inclinations. He admitted then that he often thought of a manly saying of Millet Père that it always seemed to him that suicide was the deed of a dishonest man.

During the Nuenen period he referred to Margot Begemann's attempted suicide as a 'moment of decided mania' though on the other hand he had already expressed the view 'that dying is perhaps not so difficult as living'. (358)

By the Arles period, after cutting his ear and breaking down mentally he was frequently overwhelmed emotionally and wrote occasionally to his sister and Theo about how difficult living had become and how attractive the idea of suicide was at times. Such unconscious conflicts found at this point their way into his paintings. He became obsessed with his paintings of cypresses, well-known symbols of death. Even more clearly, his painting 'The Reaper' heralds his own destruction and represents a transposition on to the canvas of his most innermost conflicts about death. He wrote to Theo, 'I see in this reaper – a vague figure fighting like a devil in the midst of the heat to get to the end of his task (as he had described himself) – I see in him the image of death . . . But there is nothing sad about his death, it goes its way in broad daylight with a sun flooding everything with a light of pure gold'. (604) As we will see he was to fire the shot that caused his death in the open fields near Auvers. When the painting was finished he wrote again in a letter of September 1889, 'The Reaper is finished . . . it is an image of death as the great book of nature speaks of it but what I have sought is the almost smiling.' (604)

On Sunday, July 27, 1890, Vincent shot himself in the fields round Auvers with a revolver. According to Tralbaut he was brought back to Auvers in the evening, where he died in Theo's arms in his room at the café, on the morning of Tuesday, July 29th. The different events and circumstances that preceded his suicide must have thrown his mind into an intolerable turmoil. By their very nature they had reactivated many of his inner conflicts to a degree that he found himself incapable of coping with.

An unfinished letter to his brother found in his pocket gave no indication of his intentions or of his reasons. This letter may well have been an incomplete draft of a letter he had been writing to Theo a few days earlier and finally decided not to send, and not the last unfinished letter to his brother as is generally assumed. This unfinished draft opens with two sentences almost identical to those which appear in the last letter that Theo actually received.[1] They read:

'There are many things I should like to write you about, but I feel it is useless. I hope you have found those worthy gentlemen favourably disposed towards you' (652, unfinished letter), while Letter 651 reads: 'Perhaps I'd rather write you about a lot of things, but to begin with the desire to do so has completely left me, and then I feel it is useless. I hope that you will have found those worthy gentlemen well disposed towards you'. (651) The unfinished draft contains some implicit criticism of Theo and it seems possible that he decided not to continue writing that letter or to send it, writing instead Letter 651 from which the critical and controversial paragraphs were suppressed. There are in the unfinished draft two passages that deserve further attention. In one he repeats an argument that he has used before on more than one occasion, that is that Theo has had his part 'in the actual production of some canvasses, which will retain their calm even in the catastrophe'. Catastrophe here may be an unconscious reference to his suicide though ostensibly it probably refers to the possibility of Theo's dismissal. This possibility seemed very likely at the time; Theo's employers were the gentlemen who, Vincent hoped, would be well disposed to Theo. We will come back to this problem shortly. The second passage occurs earlier in the letter and is connected with the first one. Theo had asked Vincent to make economies in view of the possibility of losing his post and having to become an independent dealer. He had pointed out too how difficult it was for him and his wife to raise the boy in a fourth floor flat, presumably implying that they might have to move and incur further expenses. Vincent wrote in answer to this, 'Your reassuring me as to the peacefulness of your household was hardly worth the trouble, I think, having seen the weal and woe of it

[1] Letter No. 651, *The Complete Letters*.

for myself. And I quite agree with you that rearing a boy on a fourth floor is a hell of a job for you as well as for Jo'. (652) This comment belongs in the context of a difficult complex situation that we must describe in detail in an attempt to throw further light on the conscious and unconscious determinants of Vincent's suicide.

Theo had been ill for some time and his condition had seriously deteriorated. For months he had a constant and severe cough. More important, he seems to have been suffering from a chronic nephritis, a condition that was fairly advanced at this time and progressing rapidly towards the terminal state. Theo described himself in a letter to Vincent as follows, 'As for me, I look like a corpse, but I went to see Rivet, who gave me all sorts of drugs, which at least do me enough good to put a stop to my cough, which was killing me'. (T.13) Furthermore Theo was already suffering from this condition at the time of his marriage, when he passed some remarks on the possibility of his death to which Vincent reacted strongly. It is surprising that Theo managed to carry on under the circumstances. This can have been accomplished only at the expense of great personal sacrifices. His extreme kindness, his sense of responsibility, his concern for his brother who was totally dependent on him economically and otherwise and his concern for his family at large, who were similarly dependent on him, were the inexhaustible driving forces behind him. Nevertheless at times Theo's health was so precarious that even wrtiing to his brother had to be postponed for some time, something that Vincent was bound to misinterpret according to his own fears and phantasies. Theo had written, 'I have been absolutely unable to write you sooner for the heat has been overwhelming, and I felt so weak that everything made me feel extremely tired'. (T.12) And 'I reproach myself with writing you so seldom but letter writing is extremely difficult for me lately; I don't know the reason for it'. (T.13)

To aggravate things Theo's child became ill and there was a great deal of anxiety about him with no doubt further expenses. Theo was hard put to make ends meet and expressed his concern to Vincent. 'At present we do not know what we ought to do; there are problems. Ought we to take another appartment – you know, on the first floor of the same house? Ought we to go to Auvers, to Holland, or not? Ought I to live without a thought for the morrow, and when I work all day long not to earn enough to protect that good Jo from worries over money matters, as those rats Boussod and Valadon are treating me as though I had just entered their business, and are keeping me on a short allowance? Oughtn't I to be calculating, if I spent nothing on extras and yet am short of money – oughtn't I to tell them how matters stand, and if they should dare refuse me, oughtn't I to tell them at last, Gentlemen, I am going to take the plunge, and establish myself as a private dealer in my own house?' (T.39)

Thus everybody was supposed to make economies including Vincent. Theo was doubtful that this and other difficulties could be solved. He was prepared, as we have seen, to leave his employment and if necessary to establish himself as an independent art dealer. Naturally there would be very difficult times ahead if he took that step and they all had to be prepared and economize.

Vincent was well aware of all this and expressed his concern, sympathy and support for his brother. Consciously he was frightened, unconsciously he was terrified. Theo was his only support, morally and financially. Though there was no question of Theo's withdrawing his support, he felt his whole life threatened, having to make economies involved at the least cutting down on painting materials, and perhaps having to stop painting altogether, if only temporarily – and this was the only drug that was keeping him alive. He started to wonder if Theo did not want to get rid of him, 'I feared – not altogether but yet a little – that being a burden to you, you felt me to be rather a thing to be dreaded'. (649)

He reacted automatically in the only way he knew whenever he felt he was not wanted or liked, by increasing his financial and other demands so as to feel reassured that all was well. Such behaviour was triggered off by his inner difficulties and quite independently of his conscious awareness of the difficult circumstances.

On the other hand he must have come to the conclusion that in spite of his brother's kindness the fact remained that in *reality* he was a burden to his ill brother and his family, an awareness that in Vincent's state of mind might well have contributed to his decision to commit suicide.

He himself was not too well, and on one of his visits to Theo and Jo in Paris, where he met as well several friends, he was compelled to leave Theo's house suddenly for Auvers before the arrival of Guillaumin who was coming to visit him on that day.

Dr Gachet, with all his kindness and interest in Vincent's work, was a disappointment to him. He did not feel at this point that Gachet could be counted on; he was really alone.

Another relevant set of factors concerns the illness which overcame little Vincent at this point. There was some concern for his survival and though the degree to which this was justified in reality is not clear from the letters, the fact remains that the concern was there. This is by no means surprising if we consider how heavily the death of his parents' first-born child whose name little Vincent also bore, must have loomed for Theo. As for Vincent, the birth of his nephew earlier on had reactivated many old feelings and unconscious phantasies related to the birth of his siblings and especially to that of Theo, the second boy born to the family, three years after him. These conflicts were of necessity reinforced by the special relationship that had developed in the meantime between Vincent and Theo. The latter became Father II for him and Father II was no longer satisfied with Vincent alone but had married and had given Vincent a new sibling and a rival. We have noted earlier the complexity of the impact that this event had on the artist's psychological life. Now, at this particular moment, so unfortunate in its coincidence with many other unfavourable external and internal circumstances, the child was ill, as they saw it, seriously ill. From Auvers Vincent wrote to Theo and Jo of Dr Gachet's reassurances that the child was probably only cutting his teeth and that there was no reason for concern. Nevertheless the boy's illness must have reactivated his carefully repressed aggression and his terrifying death wishes against his new competitor for Theo's help and affection. As we have mentioned, analytic experience has shown that the second child born in a family where the first one has died, always manages to find himself responsible for it in phantasy even though he might not have been born at the time. Such phantasies engender massive guilt, contribute important elements to the shape of the personality and raise enormous anxiety whenever events take place that reactivate the conflicts – such as the birth of other siblings, their illnesses, and, in adulthood, even the birth of their children. We have had already opportunity to see Vincent's anxiety in these respects in his reaction to the birth of

Christine's child while living with her in Amsterdam, and in his anxiety about Jo's pregnancy, in his reactions to death in general and more especially to the death of children. During the last few days of Vincent's life the baby was declared out of danger, a most welcome relief on the conscious level but a disappointment to his unconscious phantasies of the elimination of the rival. There can be little doubt of the terrible conflicts he had to contend with; they must have made no small contribution to his steadily growing inner turmoil, especially in his already precarious situation of mental equilibrium.

Furthermore, though Vincent was consciously resigned to a solitary life without a wife and children, Theo's marriage and the birth of the child must have reactivated his longings. We have had plenty of opportunity to see how strong these longings were and how art and the production of paintings (instead of children) were at best a really very unsatisfactory second choice for him. Theo, who was aware of Vincent's feelings, tried to console him by writing, 'I hope from the bottom of my heart that you too will some day have a wife'. (T.39)

Another important set of unconscious phantasies detectable clearly in his letters concerns his unconscious wish to appropriate for himself Jo and the little boy. This can be seen in his wanting them to come to live with him at Auvers, consciously for the sake of the health and normal development of the little one and for the sake of Jo's health. He suggested this many times, and explored several possibilities of accommodation for them at Auvers. He told them of several cases of mothers and children known to him where the move to the countryside in Auvers had worked wonders; Theo of course had to attend to his business in Paris and could not possibly have come. Furthermore, Theo was ill and looked 'like a corpse' and the idea of his possible death must have crossed Vincent's unconscious mind even if it did not reach the level of conscious awareness. Jo herself remarks in her Introductory Comments to *The Complete Letters* how much more healthy than Theo Vincent looked when she first met him on his arrival to Paris. It is by no means impossible that such comments were made openly, partly out of surprise on her part that somebody so disturbed mentally should have such a healthy appearance and partly to reassure Vincent. Be that as it may, such phantasies must have been distressing and conflictive beyond description for

Vincent, having at the same time a positive very affectionate attachment to his brother. On the other hand, he had good reasons to believe that he could not survive Theo's death and his obscure awareness of the impending possibility of this must have thrown him more into despair. To want to appropriate Theo's wife and child must in the circumstances, have raised indescribable anxiety and guilt. Yet he had experienced similar impulses in the past and had even verbalized his willingness to take Theo's mistress off his hands while they were living together in Paris. He went so far as to propose his readiness to marry her if necessary, on the pretext of liberating his brother from a troublesome relationship and burden.

It is also necessary to take into account Vincent's attraction to women who had children and who had lost their partners through death or through abandonment. He fell in love with his cousin Kee who had just become a widow and who had a little boy. He felt so strongly about her that he was unable to respect her mourning, and was reproached for his indelicacy and his untimely impulsive declaration. Later, during the Amsterdam period he was equally fascinated by Christine who had a child, was pregnant and had been 'abandoned' by the father of her children. The suffering of these women in 'mourning' was a further stimuli to his interest in them.

The obvious relationship between such pieces of manifest behaviour and his oedipal impulses needs no further elaboration here. Suffice it to say that we know of an even earlier similar phantasy where he, the young clergyman, was to take over from his father, the old clergyman.

Other no less important determinants of his suicide are related to the problem of his combined fear of failure and fear of success, which we described in a previous chapter.

Finally, as we saw in the chapter on 'The Empty Chairs', Vincent decreed his own death and even carried out the first stage of the sentence in symbolic terms by cutting his ear lobe and becoming insane. Now, under the pressure of all these factors and conflictive phantasies, he was forced to carry out the sentence fully.

Now, as before, he was unable to cope with his aggression and death wishes against Theo, against the child (as he had not been able to cope with his aggression against Gauguin, and symbolically against Theo and his father) and he was forced to turn his aggressive feelings against himself. He had to pay for his crimes in the 'talion fashion' of the unconscious. He had in phantasy, killed father, brother, nephew and friend. This time an ear lobe was not enough; he shot himself in the fields on July 27th.

Theo was called to Auvers by Dr Gachet who sent a message to him at Goupil since Vincent had refused to give him his brother's address. After his arrival he wrote to his wife:

'He was glad that I came and we are together all the time . . . poor fellow, very little happiness fell to his share, and no illusions are left him. The burden grows too heavy at times, he feels so alone. He often asks after you and the baby, and said that you could not imagine there was so much sorrow in life. Oh! if we could only give him some new courage to live. Don't get too anxious, his condition has been just as hopeless before, but his strong constitution deceived the doctors.'

According to Theo, Vincent exclaimed just before dying, 'I wish I could die now'. A few moments later his wish was granted. He was freed of his misery in the early morning of July 29, 1890. He was thirty-seven years old.

Curiously enough the words uttered by Vincent in his last moments were an exact replica of those attributed by him to Margot Begemann before her attempted suicide years earlier (see Letter 375).

It is not known for certain how he had come into possession of the gun. Some claim that it was lent to him to shoot crows in the fields near by, but I have found not sufficient confirmation of this account.

In retrospect it is not easy to establish the relative influence of each of the many factors described on the final outcome. Nevertheless it seems reasonable to assume that each contributed *per se* and through mutual reinforcement.

The account of Vincent's death would not be complete without a description of its repercussions on Theo. Theo was a broken man after his brother's suicide. To his mother he wrote, 'One cannot write how grieved one is nor find any comfort. It is a grief that will last and which I certainly shall never forget as long as I live; the only thing one might say is that he himself has the rest he was longing for . . . Life was such a burden to him; but now, as often happens, everybody is full of praise for his talents . . .

Oh Mother! he was so my own brother.' Theo's illness took a turn for the worse and his mental equilibrium gave way shortly afterwards. He followed his brother to death only six months later. Now they lie side by side in the cemetery at Auvers. And, taking his brother with him, Vincent has risen to immortality.